First World War
and Army of Occupation
War Diary
France, Belgium and Germany

30 DIVISION
Divisional Troops
Divisional Signal Company
6 November 1915 - 31 May 1919

WO95/2323/2

The Naval & Military Press Ltd
www.nmarchive.com
Published in association with The National Archives

Published by

The Naval & Military Press Ltd

Unit 10 Ridgewood Industrial Park,

Uckfield, East Sussex,

TN22 5QE England

Tel: +44 (0) 1825 749494

www.naval-military-press.com

www.nmarchive.com

This diary has been reprinted in facsimile from the original. Any imperfections are inevitably reproduced and the quality may fall short of modern type and cartographic standards.

© **Crown Copyright**
Images reproduced by permission of The National Archives, London, England, 2015.

Contents

Document type	Place/Title	Date From	Date To
Heading	WO95/2323/2 30th Divisional Sic Coy Nov 1915-May 1919		
Heading	30th Division Divl Engineers 30th Divl Sig. Coy R.E. Nov 1915-May 1919		
Heading	30th Div. Sig. Coy. Vol 1 121/7761 Nov 15 May 19		
Heading	War Diary Of The 30th Divisional Signal Company, R.E. For November, 1916		
War Diary	Larkhill	06/11/1915	06/11/1915
War Diary	Havre.	07/11/1915	07/11/1915
War Diary	Pont Remy	08/11/1915	08/11/1915
War Diary	Ailly Le Haut Clocher.	08/11/1915	17/11/1915
War Diary	Flesselles	17/11/1915	28/11/1915
War Diary	Le Meillard	28/11/1915	30/11/1915
Heading	30th Divl. Signal Coy. Vol.2 121/7928		
Heading	War Diary Of The 30th Divisional Signal Company, R.E. For December, 1915		
War Diary	Le Meillard.	01/12/1915	31/12/1915
Heading	30th Signals Vol 3 Divl.		
Heading	War Diary Of The For January 1916 1/2/16		
War Diary	Le Meillard	01/01/1916	06/01/1916
War Diary	Talmas	07/01/1916	07/01/1916
War Diary	Daours.	08/01/1916	10/01/1916
War Diary	Etinehem	11/01/1916	31/01/1916
Heading	30th Divisional Signal Coy March 1916-July 1916		
Heading	30th Signals Vol:4		
Heading	War Diary Of The 30th Divisional Signal Company, R.E. For The Month Of February 1916		
War Diary	Etinehem	01/02/1916	29/02/1916
Heading	War Diary Of The 30th Divisional Signal Company, R.E. For The Month Of March, 1916		
War Diary	Etinehem	01/03/1916	20/03/1916
War Diary	Montigny	20/03/1916	24/03/1916
War Diary	Daours.	24/03/1916	28/03/1916
War Diary	Ailly-Sur-Somme	28/03/1916	31/03/1916
Heading	War Diary Of The 30th Divisional Signal Company R.E. For The Month Of March, 1916		
War Diary	Etinehem	01/03/1916	20/03/1916
War Diary	Montigny.	20/03/1916	24/03/1916
War Diary	Daours.	24/03/1916	28/03/1916
War Diary	Sailly-Sur-Somme	28/03/1916	28/03/1916
Heading	War Diary For The Month Of April, 1916. For The 30th Divisional Signal Company-Royal Engineers.		
War Diary	Ailly-Sur-Somme	01/04/1916	30/04/1916
Heading	War Diary Of The 30th Divisional Signal Company R.E., For The Month Of May, 1916		
War Diary	Ailly-Sur-Somme	01/05/1916	03/05/1916
War Diary	Corbie	04/05/1916	04/05/1916
War Diary	Etinehem	05/05/1916	31/05/1916
Heading	War Diary Of The 30th Divisional Signal Company Royal Engineers For The Month Of June, 1916. Vol 8		

War Diary	Etinehem	01/06/1916	22/06/1916
War Diary	L.16.A.5/2	23/06/1916	30/06/1916
Heading	War Diary 30th Divisional Signal Company Royal Engineers Of The For The Month Of July. 1916		
War Diary	Bray. L.16.b.5/2	01/07/1916	03/07/1916
War Diary	Etinehem.	04/07/1916	05/07/1916
War Diary	C Copse.	06/07/1916	10/07/1916
War Diary	F Copse	11/07/1916	13/07/1916
War Diary	Etinehem	14/07/1916	14/07/1916
War Diary	Corbie	15/07/1916	19/07/1916
War Diary	Billon Farm F.24.c.4/4	19/07/1916	19/07/1916
War Diary	Citadel.	31/07/1916	31/07/1916
Miscellaneous	During the month, the Company had the following casualties:-		
Heading	30th Divisional Engineers 30th Divisional Signal Company R.E. August 1916		
Heading	War Diary Of The 30th Divisional Signal Company-Royal Engineers. For The Month Of August, 1916. Volume X.		
War Diary	Citadel.	01/08/1916	01/08/1916
War Diary	Poulainville	01/08/1916	02/08/1916
War Diary	Hallencourt	03/08/1916	04/08/1916
War Diary	Busnes.	05/08/1916	12/08/1916
War Diary	Bethune	13/08/1916	31/08/1916
Heading	War Diary Of The 30th Divisional Signal Company Royal Engineers For The Month Of September, 1916. Volume XI.		
War Diary	Bethune	01/09/1916	17/09/1916
War Diary	Doullens.	18/09/1916	20/09/1916
War Diary	Vignacourt	21/09/1916	30/09/1916
Heading	War Diary For The 30th Divisional Signal Company, Royal Engineers. For The Month Of October, 1916. Volume XII.		
War Diary	War Diary For The 30th Divisional Signal Company-Royal Engineers For The Month Of November, 1916. Volume XIII.		
War Diary	Bavincourt	01/11/1916	30/11/1916
Heading	War Diary Of The 30th Divisional Signal Company Royal Engineers For The Month Of December, 1916.Volume XIV.		
War Diary	Bavincourt	01/12/1916	31/12/1916
Heading	30 Divisional Signal Coy Jan 1917 Vol 15		
Heading	War Diary Of The 30th Divisional Signal Company-Royal Engineers For The Month Of January, 1917. Volume XV.		
War Diary	Bavincourt.	01/01/1917	06/01/1917
War Diary	Lucheux	07/01/1917	31/01/1917
War Diary	Lucheux.	07/01/1917	31/01/1917
Heading	30 Divisional Signal Coy Feb 1917 Vol 16		
Heading	War Diary Of The 30th Divisional Signal Company-Royal Engineers For The Month Of February, 1917 Volume XVI.		
War Diary	Lucheux	01/02/1917	05/02/1917
War Diary	Berneville	06/02/1917	28/02/1917
War Diary	30 Divisional Signal Coy March 1917 Vol 17		

War Diary	War Diary Of The 30th Divisional Signal Coy. R.E. For The Month Of March 1917 Volume 17		
War Diary	Berneville	02/03/1917	22/03/1917
War Diary	Bretencourt	24/03/1917	24/03/1917
Heading	30th Divisional Signal Coy April 1917 Vol 18		
Heading	War Diary Of The 30th Divisional Signal Company, R.E., For April 1917 Volume XVIII		
War Diary	Bretencourt	01/04/1917	08/04/1917
War Diary	Blairville	09/04/1917	12/04/1917
War Diary	Pommier	13/04/1917	19/04/1917
War Diary	Agny	19/04/1917	25/04/1917
War Diary	Neuville-Vitasse M18d4.2	26/04/1917	30/04/1917
Diagram etc	Draft Plan of Lines		
Miscellaneous	30th Divisional Signal Company-Royal Engineers.	07/04/1917	07/04/1917
Miscellaneous			
Miscellaneous	30th Divisional Signal Company, R.E.	24/04/1917	24/04/1917
Miscellaneous			
Heading	30th Divisional Signal Coy May 1917 Vol 19 Map No. 2 15 Dated 16/5/19 But Sheet III Refers To It. Hence Date 15 Probably 16/5/17		
Heading	War Diary Of The 30th Divisional Signal Company, Royal Engineers For May, 1917. Volume XIX.		
War Diary	Roellecourt	01/05/1917	03/05/1917
War Diary	Oeuf	03/05/1917	03/05/1917
Map	30th Division Communications 4-5-17		
War Diary	Oeuf	04/05/1917	12/05/1917
Map	War Diary 30th Division Communications No. 2		
War Diary	Oeuf	12/05/1917	15/05/1917
War Diary	Willeman	16/05/1917	21/05/1917
War Diary	Pernes	21/05/1917	22/05/1917
War Diary	Norrent Fontes	22/05/1917	23/05/1917
War Diary	Steenbecque	24/05/1917	24/05/1917
War Diary	Caestre	25/05/1917	26/05/1917
War Diary	Watou	26/05/1917	30/05/1917
War Diary	Brandhoek	30/05/1917	31/05/1917
Heading	30 Divisional Signal Coy June 1917 Vol 20		
Heading	War Diary Of The 30th Divisional Signal Company, R.E. For June 1917. Volume XX.		
War Diary	Brandhoek	01/06/1917	14/06/1917
War Diary	Reninghelst	14/06/1917	30/06/1917
Map	War Diary 30th Division Communications. 30-5-17		
Heading	30 Divisional Signal Coy July 1917 Vol 21		
Heading	War Diary Of The 30th Divisional Signal Company, R.E. For The Month Of July, 1917. Volume XXI. Vol 21		
Miscellaneous	30th Divisional Signal Company-Royal Engineers. Appendix A		
War Diary	Reninghelst	01/07/1917	06/07/1917
War Diary	Nordausque	07/07/1917	19/07/1917
War Diary	Steenvorde	19/07/1917	24/07/1917
War Diary	H27b 65.70	24/07/1917	31/07/1917
Heading	War Diary Of The 30th Divisional Signal Company For August 1917 Vol 22		
War Diary	H27b 65.70 Sheet 28 1/40000	01/08/1917	03/08/1917
War Diary	Reninghelst	04/08/1917	04/08/1917
War Diary	Godewaersvelde	05/08/1917	07/08/1917

War Diary	Merris	08/08/1917	11/08/1917
War Diary	St. Jan Cappel	12/08/1917	23/08/1917
War Diary	Ulster Camp	23/08/1917	23/08/1917
War Diary	Dranoutre	23/08/1917	31/08/1917
Heading	30th Divisional Signal Company-Royal Engineers. War Diary For The Month Of September, 1917 Volume XXIII.		
War Diary	Dranoutre	01/09/1917	30/09/1917
Heading	30th Divisional Signal Company-Royal Engineers. War Diary For The Month Of October 1917. Volume XXIV.		
War Diary	Dranoutre	01/10/1917	31/10/1917
Heading	War Diary 30th Divisional Signal Company R.E. For The Month Of November 1917. Vol 25		
War Diary	Dranoutre	01/11/1917	14/11/1917
War Diary	Steenvoorde	15/11/1917	26/11/1917
War Diary	Westoutre	27/11/1917	30/11/1917
Heading	30th Divisional Signal Company-Royal Engineers. War Diary For December 1917. Volume XXVI. Vol 26		
War Diary	Westoutre	01/12/1917	31/12/1917
Heading	30th Divisional Signal Company-Royal Engineers. War Diary For January 1918. Volume XXVII. Vol 27		
War Diary	Westoutre	01/01/1918	31/01/1918
War Diary	Rouez	01/02/1918	09/02/1918
War Diary	Ercheu	10/02/1918	22/02/1918
War Diary	Ham	23/02/1918	28/02/1918
War Diary	Dury	28/02/1918	28/02/1918
Heading	30th Divisional Signal Company-Royal Engineers. War Diary For The Month Of March 1918. Volume XXIX. Vol29		
War Diary	Dury	01/03/1918	21/03/1918
War Diary	Ham	22/03/1918	22/03/1918
War Diary	Ercheu	22/03/1918	23/03/1918
War Diary	Solente	24/03/1918	24/03/1918
War Diary	Roiglise	25/03/1918	25/03/1918
War Diary	Hangest	25/03/1918	26/03/1918
War Diary	Braches	27/03/1918	27/03/1918
War Diary	Estree-Sur-Noye	28/03/1918	29/03/1918
War Diary	St Valery-Sur-Somme	30/03/1918	31/03/1918
Heading	30th Divisional Signal Company-Royal Engineers. War Diary For The Month Of April, 1918. Volume XXX. Vol 30		
War Diary	St. Valery-Sur-Somme	01/04/1918	04/04/1918
War Diary	Proven	05/04/1918	07/04/1918
War Diary	Canal Bank	08/04/1918	12/04/1918
War Diary	Elverdinghe	13/04/1918	17/04/1918
War Diary	Busseboom	18/04/1918	26/04/1918
War Diary	Broxeele	26/04/1918	30/04/1918
Heading	30th Divisional Signal Company-Royal Engineers. War Diary For The Month Of May 1918. Volume XXXI. Vol 31		
War Diary	Broxeele	01/05/1918	14/05/1918
War Diary	Eu	15/05/1918	31/05/1918
Heading	30th Divisional Signal Company-Royal Engineers. War Diary For The Month Of June 1918. Volume XXXII.		
War Diary	Eu	01/06/1918	20/06/1918
War Diary	Rue.	21/06/1918	30/06/1918

Heading	30th Divisional Signal Company-Royal Engineers. War Diary For The Month Of July, 1918 Volume XXXIII.			
War Diary	Eperleques		01/07/1918	08/07/1918
War Diary	Cassel		09/07/1918	31/07/1918
Heading	30th Divisional Signal Company-Royal Engineers War Diary For The Month Of August 1918. Volume XXXIV.			
War Diary	Cassel		01/08/1918	10/08/1918
War Diary	Terdeghem		10/08/1918	31/08/1918
Heading	30th Divisional Signal Company-Royal Engineers. War Diary For The Month Of September 1918. Volume XXXV. Vol 35			
War Diary	Mont Vidaigne		01/09/1918	30/09/1918
Heading	30th Divisional Signal Company-Royal Engineers. War Diary For The Month Of October, 1918. Volume XXXVI. Vol 36			
War Diary	Vignacourt		02/10/1918	02/10/1918
War Diary	Allonville		03/10/1918	03/10/1918
War Diary	Buire.		04/10/1918	10/10/1918
War Diary	Fricourt.		11/10/1918	21/10/1918
War Diary	Fricourt		11/10/1918	21/10/1918
War Diary	Ribemont		22/10/1918	24/10/1918
War Diary	Talmas		25/10/1918	25/10/1918
War Diary	Pas.		26/10/1918	30/10/1918
War Diary	Bavincourt		31/10/1918	31/10/1918
War Diary	Wytschaete Area		01/10/1918	15/10/1918
War Diary	Kortewilde Area		16/10/1918	16/10/1918
War Diary	Wervicq Area		17/10/1918	18/10/1918
War Diary	Roncq and Croise		19/10/1918	19/10/1918
War Diary	Croise and Sterhoek		20/10/1918	21/10/1918
War Diary	Coyghem		22/10/1918	31/10/1918
Heading	30th Divisional Signal Company-Royal Engineers. War Diary For The Month Of November, 1918 Volume XXXVII. Vol 37			
War Diary	Rolleghem		01/11/1918	03/11/1918
War Diary	Belleghem		04/11/1918	08/11/1918
War Diary	Heestert.		09/11/1918	09/11/1918
War Diary	Watrepont		10/11/1918	10/11/1918
War Diary	Ellezelles		11/11/1918	14/11/1918
War Diary	Mouscron		15/11/1918	30/11/1918
Heading	30th Divisional Signal Company-Royal Engineers War Diary For The Month Of December, 1918. Volume XXXVIII Vol 38			
War Diary	Mouscron		01/12/1918	01/12/1918
War Diary	Renescure		02/12/1918	31/12/1918
Heading	30th. Divisional Signal Company-Royal Engineers. War Diary. For The Month Of January 1919. Volume XXXIX Vol 39			
War Diary	Renescure		01/01/1919	13/01/1919
War Diary	La Capelle		13/01/1919	14/01/1919
War Diary	Belle		15/01/1919	15/01/1919
War Diary	Colembert		16/01/1919	31/01/1919
Heading	30th Divisional Signal Company-Royal Engineers. War Diary. For The Month Of February 1919 Volume XXXX Vol 40			
War Diary	Colembert		01/02/1919	28/02/1919

Heading	30th Divisional Signal Company-Royal Engineers. War Diary For The Month Of March-1919. Volume XXXXI. Vol 41		
War Diary	Colembert	01/03/1919	12/03/1919
War Diary	Choquel	13/03/1919	15/03/1919
War Diary	Choquel (Hardelot)	16/03/1919	31/03/1919
Heading	30th Divisional Signal Company-Royal Engineers. War Diary For The Month Of April 1919. Volume XLII.		
War Diary	Choquel	01/04/1919	12/04/1919
War Diary	Condette	13/04/1919	30/04/1919
Miscellaneous	30th Divn. "A".	06/06/1919	06/06/1919
War Diary	Condette	01/05/1919	31/05/1919

WO95/
2323/2

30th Divisional Sig Coy

Nov 1915 — May 1919

**30TH DIVISION
DIVL ENGINEERS**

30TH DIVL SIG. COY R.E.
NOV 1915-MAY 1919

30th Div: Sig: Cor:
Vol I

12/7761

Nov 15
May 19

WAR DIARY

OF THE

30TH DIVISIONAL SIGNAL COMPANY, R. E.

FOR

NOVEMBER, 1915.

O.C. 30TH DIVL. SIGNAL COY. R.E.
(COUNTY PALATINE) R.E.

Army Form C. 2118.

WAR DIARY

INTELLIGENCE SUMMARY

(Erase heading not required.)

Instructions regarding War Diaries and Intelligence
Summaries are contained in F. S. Regs., Part II.
and the Staff Manual respectively. Title pages
will be prepared in manuscript.

Place	Date Novr.	Hour	Summary of Events and Information	Remarks and references to Appendices
LARKHILL	6th		Headquarters and No. 1 Sections left AMESBURY STATION by troop train at 1 p.m, embarked at SOUTHAMPTON and arrived at HAVRE about 10 a.m. on 7th November, 1915.	
HAVRE.	7th		Disembarked at HAVRE 7 a.m. and proceeded to No. 5 Rest Camp. Entrained at 11 p.m. at Point 4 GARE DES MARCHANDISES.	
PONT REMY	8th		Arrived PONT REMY at 3 p.m. Detrained and marched to AILLY LE HAUT CLOCHER.	
AILLY LE HAUT CLOCHER.	8th to 17th		Arrived AILLY LE HAUT CLOCHER at 8 p.m. Went into billets. Established communication to 89th Bde. at FRAINGIRES; 90th Bde. at ST. RIQUIER; and 91st Bde. at GORENFLOS. No other events occured worthy of record.	
FLESSELLES	17th to 28th		Left AILLY at 8-30 a.m. on 17th November, 1915 and proceeded to new billets at FLESSELLES. Billeting arrangements at first not satisfactory owing to the fact that certain portions of 26th Division had not yet left. Lines were laid to VAUX, MONTON VILLERS AND MOLLIENS. Remained at FLESSELLES till 28th November, 1915.	
LE MEILLARD	28th to 30th.		Left FLESSELLES at 8-30 a.m. and proceeded to new billets at LE MEILLARD. Communication was established with the Artillery at ST. OUEN; 89th Bde. at RIBEACOURT, 90th Bde. at CANAPLES; and 91st Bde. at FIENVILLERS.	

30th Bttl: Signal Coz:
Vol: 2

1948
to
1954

WAR DIARY

OF THE

30TH DIVISIONAL SIGNAL COMPANY, R. E.

FOR

DECEMBER, 1915.

31-12-15.

Army Form C. 2118

WAR DIARY
INTELLIGENCE SUMMARY

(Erase heading not required.)

Instructions regarding War Diaries and Intelligence Summaries are contained in F. S. Regs., Part II. and the Staff Manual respectively. Title pages will be prepared in manuscript.

Place	Date	Hour	Summary of Events and Information	Remarks and references to Appendices
LE MEILLARD.	Decr. 1st to 31st		Nothing worthy of record occured until the 19th December, 1915, when the 21st Brigade Signal Section joined this Division, taking the place of the 91st Brigade Signal Section at FIENVILLERS, who joined the 7th Division on the same day. On the 26th December, 1915, communication was re-established with the 89th Brigade at RIBEAUCOURT, who had returned from trench training.	

30 = Serials
— vol 3

War Diary of the

for January. 1916.

O.C. 30TH DIVL. SIGNAL COY. R.E.

Army Form C. 2118.

WAR DIARY
&
INTELLIGENCE SUMMARY.
(Erase heading not required.)

Instructions regarding War Diaries and Intelligence Summaries are contained in F. S. Regs., Part II. and the Staff Manual respectively. Title pages will be prepared in manuscript.

Place	Date	Hour	Summary of Events and Information	Remarks and references to Appendices
LE MEILLARD	1st to 6th	—	Notification received that No. 81688 - Pioneer E. Furness had been accidentally killed by a motor lorry passing over him at 11-45 a.m. on the 31st December, 1915.	
TALMAS	7th	—	Left LE MEILLARD at 8-30 a.m. on the 7th instant, arriving at TALMAS on the same day at about 2 p.m., where the Company went into billets and stayed over night. A small party remained behind at LE MEILLARD.	
DAOURS.	8th to 10th.	—	Left TALMAS at 8-30 a.m. on the 8th instant and arrived at DAOURS at 3 p.m., where the Company went into billets. An office was opened at DAOURS at 4 p.m. The party left behind at LE MEILLARD closed down at 4 p.m., arriving at DAOURS at 6 p.m.	
ETINEHEM	11th	—	Headquarters Section left DAOURS at 9-30 p.m. on the 11th instant, arriving at ETINEHEM at about 1 p.m. the same day.	
"	12th	—	No. 1 Section followed leaving DAOURS on the 12th instant at 8-30 a.m. arriving about 1 p.m.	
"	"	12 ndon.	The Signal Office was taken over from the 5th Divl. Signal Company	
"	13th to 27th.	—	On the 17th instant Portable Electric Light Set was received. During this period nothing further occured worthy of record.	
"	28th	a.m. 8-30	All lines to 90th Bde. at SUZANNE cut by shell fire.	

Army Form C. 2118.

WAR DIARY
INTELLIGENCE SUMMARY

(Erase heading not required.)

Instructions regarding War Diaries and Intelligence Summaries are contained in F. S. Regs., Part II. and the Staff Manual respectively. Title pages will be prepared in manuscript.

Place	Date	Hour	Summary of Events and Information	Remarks and references to Appendices
ETINEHEM	28th	12 noon.	One man of No. 3 Section attached to 90th Bde. slightly wounded.	
"	"	12 noon to 5 p.m.	Cable Wagon No. 1 under Lieut. Hindle, having repaired the previous break, continued on to SUZANNE repairing breaks as they occured.	
"	"	3-30	Cable in river for C.R.A. to Right Group cut. Cause unknown.	
"	"	4-30	Cable Wagon No. 1 laid line from SUZANNE to DRAGONS WOOD. Nearly all the Brigade lines forward were cut and repaired.	
"	"	10-0	Cable Wagon No. 2 under Sergt. Haworth left to lay line to SUZANNE from cross roads at BRAY. They lost their way in the fog. In touch with Signal Office at intervals only.	
"	"	10-30	Communication by wire restored to 90th Bde.	
			In the meantime the service was kept up by Despatch Rider during a heavy bombardment with lachrymatory and high explosive shells. Despatch Riders and Linesmen did excellent work under very trying conditions. Three of the breaks appeared to be clean cuts and not due to shell fire.	
"	29th	4 a.m.	Cable Wagon No. 2 under Sergt. Haworth arrived at SUZANNE. Line through.	
			Activity went on all night. No more lines were cut.	
"	"	8 a.m.	Cable Party reported back from laying line from BRAY to SUZANNE.	
"	"	9 a.m.	Line laid by Cable Wagon No. 2 cut by shell fire in the region of CAPPY.	
"	"	3 p.m.	Receiving 8 miles of cable from 10th Corps.	

Army Form C. 2118.

WAR DIARY
or
INTELLIGENCE SUMMARY.

(Erase heading not required.)

Instructions regarding War Diaries and Intelligence Summaries are contained in F. S. Regs., Part II. and the Staff Manual respectively. Title pages will be prepared in manuscript.

Place	Date	Hour	Summary of Events and Information	Remarks and references to Appendices
ETINEHEM	Mar. 29th	p.m. 7-30	River line cut in the region of CAPPY by shell fire.	
"	"	9-0	Heavy bombardment by French SOUTH of SOMME.	
"	"	10-0	Very heavy traffic. Necessary to add an instrument to 10th Corps telephone lines to cope with it.	
"	30th	1 a.m.	Zeppelin reported over A. and B. Sectors.	
"	"	9 a.m.	Buried line to SUZANNE cut. Found to have direct hit on test box near BRONFAY dug out.	
"	"	10-30 a.m.	Communication to SUZANNE via BRONFAY dug out restored.	
"	31st	11 a.m.	BRONFAY dug out line to SUZANNE converted into right and left group line for telephone lines to SUZANNE via ordinary route restored, one being used for speaking and the other for telegraph working.	
"	"	5-30 p.m.	Received Gas warning from 18th Division. Passed forward to all Units.	

30th Divisional Signal Coy

March 1916 – July 1916

30th Septr 50
Vol: 4

WAR DIARY

OF THE

30TH DIVISIONAL SIGNAL COMPANY, R. E.

FOR THE

MONTH OF

FEBRUARY, 1916.

[signature] Lieut. R.E.
O.C. 30TH DIVL. SIGNAL COY. R.E.

1-3-16.

Army Form C. 2118

WAR DIARY

~~INTELLIGENCE SUMMARY~~

(Erase heading not required.)

Instructions regarding War Diaries and Intelligence Summaries are contained in F.S. Regs., Part II. and the Staff Manual respectively. Title Pages will be prepared in manuscript.

Place	Date	Hour	Summary of Events and Information	Remarks and references to Appendices
ETINEHEM.	1st	—	Officer's charger allotted to Officer i/c Signals, 90th Infty. Bde. killed. Two Other Ranks wounded.	
"	2nd.	—	3 Other ranks of No. 4 Section attached 21st Infty. Bde. wounded.	
"	3rd to 29th.		During this period nothing occured worthy of record. There have been a large number of minor breakages of wires, but no difficulty has been experienced in keeping up communication with the various units.	

1875 Wt. W⁵593/826 1,000,000 4/15 J.B.C. & A. A.D.S.S./Forms/C. 2118.

30 Div
1) Signal
March
Vol 5

WAR DIARY
OF THE
30TH DIVISIONAL SIGNAL COMPANY, R. E.
FOR THE
MONTH OF
MARCH, 1916.

Army Form C. 2118

WAR DIARY

~~INTELLIGENCE~~ SUMMARY

(Erase heading not required.)

Instructions regarding War Diaries and Intelligence Summaries are contained in F.S. Regs., Part II. and the Staff Manual respectively. Title Pages will be prepared in manuscript.

Place	Date 1916	Hour	Summary of Events and Information	Remarks and references to Appendices
ETINEHEM	1st to 20th.		Communication at all times was well maintained. Much work was done in connection with the burying of forward lines.	
"			The 18th Divisional Signal Company took over the Office at 12 noon on the 20th instant.	
MONTIGNY	20th to 24th.		Office opened at MONTIGNY at 12 noon on the 20th instant. Visual communication was established, but much difficulty was experienced owing to mist. This Office was closed down at 11 a.m. on the 24th instant.	
DAOURS.	24th to 28th.		Office opened at DAOURS at 11 a.m. on the 24th instant. Nothing worthy of record occurred. This office was closed at 12 noon on the 28th instant.	
AILLY-SUR-SOMME.	28th to 31st		Office opened at AILLY-SUR-SOMME at 12 noon on the 28th instant. Visual communication was established to the 90th Bde. at CORBIE. Very great difficulty was experienced in getting suitable billets for the men and horse standings. On the 28th instant, Corporal Holden, Motor Cyclist of this Unit, collided with a motor ambulance sustaining serious injuries.	

1875. Wt. W 593/826 1,000,000 4/15 J.B.C. & A. A.D.S.S./Forms/C. 2118.

WAR OF THE DIARY

30TH DIVISIONAL SIGNAL COMPANY R. E.

FOR THE MONTH OF MARCH, 1916.

[signature] Capt.
O.C. 30TH DIVL. SIGNAL COY. R.E.

31-3-16.

Army Form C. 2118

WAR DIARY
or
INTELLIGENCE SUMMARY

(Erase heading not required.)

Instructions regarding War Diaries and Intelligence Summaries are contained in F. S. Regs., Part II. and the Staff Manual respectively. Title Pages will be prepared in manuscript.

Place	Date	Hour	Summary of Events and Information	Remarks and references to Appendices
ETINEHEM	1916. 1st to 20th.	-	Communication at all times was well maintained. Much work was done in connection with the burying of forward lines.	
"	"	-	The 18th Divisional Signal Company took over the Office at 12 noon on the 20th instant. Visual communication was established, but much difficulty was experienced owing to mist.	
MONTIGNY.	20th to 24th.	-	Office opened at MONTIGNY at 12 noon on the 20th instant. Visual communication was established, but much difficulty was experienced owing to mist.	
			This Office was closed down at 11 noon on the 24th instant.	
DAOURS.	24th to 28th.		Office opened at DAOURS at 11 a.m. on the 24th instant. Nothing worthy of record occured.	
			This Office was closed at 12 noon on the 28th instant.	
AILLY-SUR-SOMME.	28th to		Office opened at AILLY-SUR-SOMME at 12 noon on the 28th instant. Visual communication was established to the 90th Bde. at CORBIE.	
			Very great difficulty was experienced in getting suitable billets for the men, and horse standings.	
			On the 28th instant, Corporal Holden, Motor Cyclist, of this Unit, collided with a motor ambulance sustaining serious injuries.	

1875 Wt. W593/826 1,000,000 4/15 J.B.C. & A. A.D.S.S./Forms/C. 2118.

R.E. 30 Div
vol 6

WAR DIARY

FOR THE MONTH OF

APRIL, 1916.

FOR THE

30th DIVISIONAL SIGNAL COMPANY - ROYAL ENGINEERS.

[signature]
Capt. R.E.
O.C. 30TH DIVL SIGNAL COY.
R.E.

Army Form C. 2118

WAR DIARY
INTELLIGENCE SUMMARY
(Erase heading not required.)

Instructions regarding War Diaries and Intelligence Summaries are contained in F. S. Regs., Part II. and the Staff Manual respectively. Title Pages will be prepared in manuscript.

Place	Date	Hour	Summary of Events and Information	Remarks and references to Appendices
AILLY-SUR-SOMME.	1st to 30th.	—	On the 7th instant No. M2/051624 - Private H. Broadbent, M.T.- A.S.C. attached to this Unit, was accidentally killed on duty whilst riding a motor cycle. Up to the 10th instant communication by means of visual signalling was carried on, and proved good training. A station was worked from here to CORBIE, a distance of about 15 miles, but had to be closed down after two days owing to bad weather. During the month experiments in signalling were carried out with No. 9 Royal Flying Squadron, which proved quite successful. We demonstrated the use of electric signalling lamp between aeroplane and earth and vice-versa. This should prove most useful in the event of an advance, as isolated units would be able to give their position to aeroplanes who would return to Headquarters with the information. On the 26th instant leave re-opened. On the 28th instant visited ETINEHEM and discussed communications during the relief.	

30 Div Signals Vol 7

WAR DIARY

OF THE

30TH DIVISIONAL SIGNAL COMPANY R. E.,

FOR THE MONTH

OF

MAY, 1916.

[signature] Captain.

1-6-16.

Army Form C. 2118

WAR DIARY
~~INTELLIGENCE~~ SUMMARY

(Erase heading not required.)

Instructions regarding War Diaries and Intelligence Summaries are contained in F. S. Regs., Part II. and the Staff Manual respectively. Title Pages will be prepared in manuscript.

Place	Date	Hour	Summary of Events and Information	Remarks and references to Appendices
AILLY-SUR-SOMME.	1st to 3rd.		During this period nothing worthy of record occurred.	
CORBIE	4th		Headquarters and No. 1 Section left AILLY-SUR SOMME at 8-30 a.m. on the 4th instant arriving at CORBIE at about 5 p.m. the same day, where billets were obtained for the night.	
ETINEHEM	5th to 27th		Headquarters and No. 1 Sections resumed the journey to ETINEHEM, starting from CORBIE at 7-30 a.m. on the 5th instant and arriving at ETINEHEM about 10 a.m. on the same day, at which place billets and horse standings were obtained.	
			The Signal Office was taken over from the 18th Divisional Signal Company at 11 a.m. on the 5th instant.	
"	28th		Owing to the mules in the Ration Wagon taking fright and bolting, No. 85386 C.Q.M.S. Jackson, C. of this Unit sustained injuries which necessitated his removal to the Field Ambulance.	
"	to 31st		A great amount of work has been done during the month in the burying of new lines.	
			Communication at all times was well maintained.	

30 Div
Signals
June
Vol 8

WAR DIARY

OF THE

30TH DIVISIONAL SIGNAL COMPANY ROYAL ENGINEERS

FOR THE

MONTH OF

JUNE, 1916.

Army Form C. 2118

WAR DIARY
INTELLIGENCE SUMMARY
(Erase heading not required.)

Instructions regarding War Diaries and Intelligence Summaries are contained in F. S. Regs., Part II. and the Staff Manual respectively. Title Pages will be prepared in manuscript.

Place	Date	Hour	Summary of Events and Information	Remarks and references to Appendices
ETINEHEM	1st to 22nd		During this period a large amount of work was done in connection with the laying of buried lines and river lines. The latter work was considerably delayed owing to the frequent damage caused to the lines by French soldiers fishing by means of bombs. The matter was reported to the French authorities, but this had no effect. On the 15th instant a H.E. shell dropped in our encampment, causing 3 Other Rank casualties (2 severely wounded, 1 since died of wounds, and 1 slightly wounded returned to duty) and killing 4 horses and 2 mules and wounding 10 other animals.	
L.16.b.5/2	23rd to 30th		On the 23rd instant Headquarters were moved to our Battle Headquarters L.16.b.5/2, a point N.W. of BRAY, a sub-office being kept on at ETINEHEM for "Q" Branch work and pigeon work. On the 30th instant 1 Other Rank employed on Corps Intelligence work in the front line was wounded. From the time of taking up our position at Battle Headquarters to the end of the month no difficulty was experienced in keeping up communication with all Brigades and Units.	

30/ July
Signals
Vol 9

WAR DIARY
OF THE

FOR THE MONTH OF
JULY, 1916.

J. Mulso mulls
Capt. R.E.
O.C. 30TH DIVL. SIGNAL COY.
R.E.

Army Form C. 2118

WAR DIARY

~~INTELLIGENCE SUMMARY~~

(Erase heading not required.)

Instructions regarding War Diaries and Intelligence Summaries are contained in F. S. Regs., Part II. and the Staff Manual respectively. Title Pages will be prepared in manuscript.

Place	Date	Hour	Summary of Events and Information	Remarks and references to Appendices
BRAY. L.16.b.5/2.	1st to 3rd		On the 1st the Advanced Divisional Headquarter Office (Battle Headquarters) was at the BRAY DUGOUTS (L.16.b.5/2). An Office was maintained at ETINEHEM for "Q" Branch work and also as an alternative route to Corps. Our transport lines were at ETINEHEM. During the battle on the 1st communication was well maintained. Very few of the Brigade lines were cut and any that were cut were at once transferred on to the alternative routes. The lines forward of Brigades were mostly buried below communication trenches at a depth of 6" to 8". The lines that were taken over by the first wave were not satisfactory, but those laid after the objective had been reached were good, but it was found necessary to place linesmen at close intervals along the cable route for rapid maintenance. The pigeon service during the whole of the battle was excellent. Visual communication was good. The light French lamp proved most practicable and superior to the Flying Corps lamp which is heavy and very easily goes out of action. A visual station placed South of the PERONNE ROAD picked up many S.O.S. calls and messages. The first message received after our troops entry into MONTAUBAN was by pigeon post, the time taken being 23 minutes.	
ETINEHEM.	4th to 5th.		The 9th Divisional Signal Company took over the Office at the BRAY DUGOUTS at 10 a.m. on the 4th. We still maintained the Office at ETINEHEM (Divisional Headquarters).	
C COPSE.	6th to 10th.		An Advanced Office was opened at "C" Copse on the 6th.	
F COPSE.	11th to 13th.		The Advanced Office was moved to F. Copse on the 11th. During the operations from the 7th to the 13th it was necessary to build several new lines. Lines were continually being cut by shell-fire and the line to TRONES WOOD was almost impossible to maintain. Visual signalling and pigeons were used with success.	

1875 Wt. W593/826 1,000,000 4/15 J.B.C. & A. A.D.S.S./Forms/C. 2118.

Army Form C. 2118

WAR DIARY
or
INTELLIGENCE SUMMARY

Sheet 2.

(Erase heading not required.)

Instructions regarding War Diaries and Intelligence Summaries are contained in F.S. Regs., Part II. and the Staff Manual respectively. Title Pages will be prepared in manuscript.

Place	Date	Hour	Summary of Events and Information	Remarks and references to Appendices
ETINEHEM	14th		The 18th Divisional Signal Company took over the Office at "F" Copse on the 14th., the whole of our Company returning to ETINEHEM (Divisional Headquarters).	
CORBIE	15th to 19th.		The whole of Headquarters and No. 1 Section moved to CORBIE on the 15th instant.	
BILLON FARM F.24.c.4/4.			Headquarters and No. 1 Section moved to Billon Farm (F.24.c.4/4), with the transport lines below BRONFAY FARM. The Advanced Divisional Office was at F.24.c.4/4.	
			For the operation on the 23rd so little time was available for the erection of lines that it was necessary for most of them to be poled cable. The lines between the Division and the Brigade held fairly well considering their exposed position. Communication by wire forward of the Advanced Brigade Headquarters was not very satisfactory, the wires for the most part being cut as they were laid. Communication was established between the Advanced Brigade Headquarters and Battalions by "runner". The visual system was not made use of. Pigeons were satisfactory but liberated too early, the birds taking some time to get back.	
CITADEL.	31st		The 55th Divisional Signal Company took over the Office at F.24.c.4/4 on the morning of the 31st. Transport lines still below BRONFAY FARM.	
			An Office was opened at the CITADEL on the morning of the 31st.	
			For the operation on the 30th a cable trench 6 feet deep was dug from the old German front line to the BRICQUETERIE with a tee off to TRAIN ALLEY. The cables in this main cable trench leading to the BRICQUETERIE were all cut owing to an ammunition dump being set on fire and it was impossible to get near the break for some time. This was very unfortunate as it occurred just after the attack had been launched. Visual signalling and pigeons were of no use owing to the heavy mist. 3 Wireless stations were erected but were not made use of.	

Army Form C. 2118

WAR DIARY
or
INTELLIGENCE SUMMARY
(Erase heading not required.)

Instructions regarding War Diaries and Intelligence Summaries are contained in F. S. Regs., Part II. and the Staff Manual respectively. Title Pages. will be prepared in manuscript.

Place	Date	Hour	Summary of Events and Information	Remarks and references to Appendices
			During the month, the Company had the following casualties:—	
	8th.		1 Other Rank wounded (artillery fire)	
	9th.		1 " killed "	
	10th.		1 " wounded and 1 Other Rank killed (artillery fire).	
	21st.		1 " (20th King's Liverpool Regiment) attached this Unit killed (artillery fire	
	"		1 " wounded (artillery fire).	
	23rd.		3 " " and 3 Other Ranks killed (artillery fire),	
	30th.		9 " " (8 by aeroplane bombs and 1 artillery fire) and 1 Other Rank killed (aeroplane bomb).	

30th Divisional Engineers

30th DIVISIONAL SIGNAL COMPANY. R.E.

AUGUST 1916

Signals Vol 10

SECRET.

WAR DIARY

OF THE 30TH DIVISIONAL SIGNAL COMPANY - ROYAL ENGINEERS.

FOR THE MONTH OF AUGUST, 1916.

VOLUME X.

4-9-16.

Capt.
O.C. 30TH DIVL. SIGNAL COY.
R.E.

Army Form C. 2118

WAR DIARY
or
INTELLIGENCE SUMMARY

(Erase heading not required.)

Instructions regarding War Diaries and Intelligence Summaries are contained in F. S. Regs., Part II. and the Staff Manual respectively. Title Pages will be prepared in manuscript.

Place	Date	Hour	Summary of Events and Information	Remarks and references to Appendices
CITADEL.	1st		The Office at the CITADEL was taken over by the 24th Divisional Signal Company at 10 p.m. on the 1st.	
POULAINVILLE	1st.		Transport left BRONFAY at 8-30 a.m. on the 1st and halted at POULAINVILLE at 6 p.m., where the Company stayed overnight.	
"	2nd.		Transport resumed journey from POULAINVILLE at 8-30 a.m. on the 2nd, arriving at HALLENCOURT at 4 p.m. ~~where the Company stayed overnight~~.	
HALLENCOURT	3rd to 4th.		Headquarters and No. 1 Sections left HALLENCOURT at 8-30 a.m. on the 4th for LONGPRE for entrainment to BERGUETTE. BERGUETTE was reached at 6 p.m., where the Company detrained, afterwards proceeding by road to BUSNES, arriving there at 8 p.m. on the 4th., where the Company went into billets.	
BUSNES.	5th to 12th.		Nothing worthy of record occurred during this period.	
			Headquarters & No. 1 Sections left BUSNES at 6 a.m. on the 12th, arriving at BETHUNE at 11 a.m., where the Company went into billets.	
BETHUNE	13th to 31st.		A sub-office was established at LOCON on the 13th.	
			From the 14th to the 28th, linemen were engaged on constructing a buried cable system from CANAL HOUSE to GIVENCHY KEEP. This route is 7-feet deep and contains 20 pairs.	

Vol II

SECRET.

WAR DIARY
OF THE 30TH DIVISIONAL SIGNAL COMPANY, ROYAL ENGINEERS
FOR THE MONTH OF SEPTEMBER, 1916.
VOLUME XI.

3-10-16.

Capt.
O.C. 30TH DIVL. SIGNAL COY. R.E.

Army Form C. 2118

WAR DIARY
or
INTELLIGENCE SUMMARY
(Erase heading not required.)

Instructions regarding War Diaries and Intelligence Summaries are contained in F.S. Regs., Part II. and the Staff Manual respectively. Title Pages will be prepared in manuscript.

Place	Date	Hour	Summary of Events and Information	Remarks and references to Appendices
BETHUNE	1st to 11th	—	Nothing worthy of record occurred during this period.	
"	12th.		7-feet cable trench from CANAL HOUSE to GIVENCHY completed. Detachment of telegraph operators and linemen under Lieut. W.R.Allen, R.E. left on the 12th instant for duty with XVIIth Corps at AUBIGNY.	
"	17th.		Detachment of telegraph operators and linemen under Lieut. W.R.Allen, R.E. returned from duty with XVIIth Corps.	
DOULLENS.	18th to 20th.		H.Q. and No. 1 Section (less 1 Cable Section) left BETHUNE at 8-45 a.m. on the 18th instant for entrainment at FOUQUEREUIL. 1 Cable Section under Lieut. W.R.Allen, R.E. left behind at BETHUNE with 30th Divisional Artillery. Company detrained at DOULLENS, where they went into billets.	
VIGNACOURT	21st to 30th.		H.Q. & No. 1 Section (less 1 Cable Section) left DOULLENS at 9 a.m. on the 21st instant, arriving at VIGNACOURT at 12-30 p.m. the same day, where the Company went into billets. Very poor accommodation for men. Nothing else occurred worthy of record.	

Vol 12

SECRET.

WAR DIARY
FOR THE
30TH DIVISIONAL SIGNAL COMPANY, ROYAL ENGINEERS.
FOR THE
MONTH OF
OCTOBER, 1916.
VOLUME XII.

4-11-16.

[signature]
Capt. R.E.
30TH DIVL. SIGNAL COY.
R.E.

SECRET.

WAR DIARY
FOR THE
30TH DIVISIONAL SIGNAL COMPANY - ROYAL ENGINEERS
FOR THE MONTH OF
NOVEMBER, 1916.
VOLUME XIII.

Capt. R.E.
O.C. 30TH DIVL SIGNAL COY.

Army Form C. 2118

WAR DIARY

~~INTELLIGENCE~~ SUMMARY

(Erase heading not required.)

Instructions regarding War Diaries and Intelligence Summaries are contained in F. S. Regs., Part II. and the Staff Manual respectively. Title Pages will be prepared in manuscript.

Place	Date	Hour	Summary of Events and Information	Remarks and references to Appendices
BAVINCOURT	1st to 17th.		On the 14th instant, the Cable Section of this Unit detached with the 30th Divisional Artillery sustained the following casualties through shell-fire:- 3 Other Ranks Killed. 3 Other Ranks Wounded. 1 Riding Horse Killed.	
"	18th to 25th.		No. 2 Section of this Unit, attached 89th Infantry Brigade, moved its Office from POMMIER to LA CAUCHIE on the 18th instant.	
"	26th to 30th.		The Cable Section detached with 30th Divisional Artillery rejoined Unit on the 26th instant. During the month 3 men of the Cable Section detached with 30th Divisional Artillery were awarded the Military Medal. No difficulty was experienced in keeping up communication during the whole of the month. Nothing else worthy of record occurred.	

SECRET.

Vol 14

WAR DIARY
OF THE
30TH DIVISIONAL SIGNAL COMPANY
ROYAL ENGINEERS
FOR THE
MONTH OF DECEMBER, 1916.

VOLUME XIV.

N.E.Baker
11 Lieut. R.E.
for Captain.   R.E.
O.C. 30TH DIVL. SIGNAL COY.
                                R.E.

Army Form C. 2118

WAR DIARY

~~INTELLIGENCE SUMMARY~~

(*Erase heading not required.*)

Instructions regarding War Diaries and Intelligence Summaries are contained in F. S. Regs., Part II. and the Staff Manual respectively. Title Pages will be prepared in manuscript.

Place	Date	Hour	Summary of Events and Information	Remarks and references to Appendices
BAVINCOURT	1st to 13th.	—	During this period, nothing worthy of record occurred.	
"	14th to 29th.		A system of "Position Calls" was established throughout the Divisional Area on the 14th instant.	
"	30th to 31st.		The visual signalling system of the Divisional Section was tested on the 30th instant, neither telephonic nor telegraphic communication being employed between the hours of 9 a.m. and 4 p.m. on that day. The Company spent a very Happy X'mas. No difficulty was experienced in keeping up communications during the month.	

3o Divisional Signal Coy

Jan 1917

Vol 15

SECRET.

WAR DIARY
OF THE
30TH DIVISIONAL SIGNAL COMPANY - ROYAL ENGINEERS
FOR THE MONTH
OF
JANUARY, 1917.

VOLUME XV.

[signature]
Captain. R.E.
O.C. 30TH DIVL. SIGNAL COY. R.E.

WAR DIARY

INTELLIGENCE SUMMARY

Army Form C. 2118

Place	Date	Hour	Summary of Events and Information	Remarks and references to Appendices
BAVINCOURT.	1st to 6th.		Captain MOLESWORTH, J.D.N. awarded Military Cross. (London Gazette dated 3-1-17. Lieut. McGowan, G. Mentioned in Despatches (L.G.d/3-1-17). Office at BAVINCOURT taken over by the 49th Divisional Signal Company R.E. on the 7th instant.	
LUCHEUX.	7th to 31st.		H.Q. & No. 1 Sections moved from BAVINCOURT to LUCHEUX on the 7th instant, starting from BAVINCOURT at 9 a.m. arriving at LUCHEUX at 2 p.m., where the Company went into billets. The billets were very poor indeed. On the 11th instant, the H.Q., No.s. 1,2,3 and 4 Sections concentrated for training. Classes were arranged for a thorough training in all Signal Service work, particular attention being paid to visual signalling; manipulation, adjustment. and care of the Fullerphone; and lineman's duties. Physical Drill and Squad Drill were also included in the daily programme as a means of raising the standard of discipline. 39 Infantry and 30 Artillery Signallers also took part in the Training Scheme. The Course extended over a period of 14 days, when the Brigade Sections returned to their respective Brigade areas. The Course proved highly satisfactory. During the period of concentration, the whole of the Company stores, harness and transport were thoroughly overhauled.	

Army Form C. 2118

Sheet 2

WAR DIARY
INTELLIGENCE SUMMARY
(Erase heading not required.)

Instructions regarding War Diaries and Intelligence Summaries are contained in F. S. Regs., Part II. and the Staff Manual respectively. Title Pages will be prepared in manuscript.

Place	Date	Hour	Summary of Events and Information	Remarks and references to Appendices
LUCHEUX.	7th to 31st.		On the 18th instant 1 Officer and 11 O.Rs. this Unit left for attachment to XVIIth Corps Signals for work on Cable Trenches in that Corps area.	

3º Divisional Signal Coy

Feb 1917

Vol 16

SECRET.

WAR DIARY
OF THE
30TH DIVISIONAL SIGNAL COMPANY – ROYAL ENGINEERS
FOR THE
MONTH OF
FEBRUARY, 1917.
VOLUME XVI.

4-3-17.

B Howorth
Captain. R.E.
O.C. 30TH DIVL. SIGNAL COY.
R.E.

Army Form C. 2118

WAR DIARY
or
INTELLIGENCE SUMMARY
(Erase heading not required.)

Instructions regarding War Diaries and Intelligence Summaries are contained in F. S. Regs., Part II. and the Staff Manual respectively. Title Pages will be prepared in manuscript.

Place	Date	Hour	Summary of Events and Information	Remarks and references to Appendices
LUCHEUX	1st to 5th.		During this period nothing worthy of record occurred	
BERNEVILLE	6th to 28th.		Headquarters & No. 1 Sections left LUCHEUX at 9-30 a.m., arriving at BERNEVILLE at 3-30 p.m., where they went into billets.	
			2nd Lieut. Mortimer, R.E. admitted to hospital on 20th instant.	
			Captain B.HOWORTH, R.E. took up command vice Captain J.D.N.MOLESWORTH, R.E. to Heavy Branch Machine Gun Corps 22-2-17.	
			Captain J.D.N. MOLESWORTH, R.E. left on the 23rd instant.	
			Captain E. HINDLE R.E., left for G.H.Q. Wireless Course 27-2-17.	
			Lieut. J.G. ALLEN, 19th King's Liverpool Regiment, joined for temporary duty 27-2-17.	
			From the 13th instant, all linemen have been employed in burying cables in front of Brigade Battle Headquarters and between Brigades.	
			From 27th instant, small party engaged on clearing up derelict cables in and around the village. Several miles of good cable recovered.	
			6-pair airline from BERNEVILLE towards the Divisional O.P. (R.11.b.8.9.) continued.	

1875. Wt. W593/826 1,000,000 4/15 J.B.C. & A. A.D.S.S./Forms/C. 2118.

30 Divisional Signal Coy

March 1917

Vol 17

SECRET.

1917

WAR DIARY

OF THE

30TH DIVISIONAL SIGNAL COY. R.E.

FOR THE MONTH OF

MARCH 1917.

VOLUMNE 17.

4.4.17.

Capt. R.E.
O.C. 30TH DIVL. SIGNAL COY. R.E.

Army Form C. 2118

WAR DIARY
or
INTELLIGENCE SUMMARY
(Erase heading not required.)

Instructions regarding War Diaries and Intelligence Summaries are contained in F.S. Regs., Part II. and the Staff Manual respectively. Title Pages will be prepared in manuscript.

Place	Date	Hour	Summary of Events and Information	Remarks and references to Appendices
Bruneville	2nd.		2nd. Lieut. B.F. Mortimer evacuated to England.	
	5th.		Capt. Hindle rejoined company after attending Wireless course at G.H.Q.	
	10th.		89th Bde. took over from 21st Bde. and held the front formerly held by the two Brigades. 21st. Bde. Hqrs. moved back to Simencourt.	
			From the beginning of the month to the 18th. large infantry working-parties were employed daily digging cable-trenches for the buried system on the Division front. Routes forward from MQ a 5·8 [21st. Bde. Advr. Hqrs.] and from M8 a 7·0 [89th Bde. Advr. Hqrs.] were completed, and also a lateral route between these two points. Another route was commenced, backwards from 89th Bde. Advr. Hqrs. to Dir O.P. [R11 b 8·9], for communication between Bde. Hqrs. and Bde. Hqrs. Three quarters of this route were completed by Mar. 18th., when all work on these cable-trenches ceased owing to the enemy evacuating their line.	
	18th.		89th Bde. Hqrs. moved into this advanced position.	
	22nd.		90th Bde. Hqrs. moved from MC 7·0 to Blamont Farm.	
Bretencourt.	24th.		Div. Hqrs. moved to Bretencourt: office established at Bretencourt Chateau.	

30TH Divisional Signal Coy

April 1917

Vol 18

Secret.

Vol 18

War Diary

of the

30th Divisional Signal Company, R.E.

for ~~the~~

April 1917.

VOLUME XVIII

WAR DIARY
or
INTELLIGENCE SUMMARY
(Erase heading not required.)

Army Form C. 2118

S.W.I. I

Place	Date	Hour	Summary of Events and Information	Remarks and references to Appendices
BRETENCOURT	April 1st		All linesmen employed on building a main 6 pair airline forward from Div H.Q. to BLAIRVILLE and on to Bac Hops on to railway cutting S3c also put through certain German buried route to Blettys	S3c S15SW
	2nd		Work on airline continued. 2/Lieg. SCATTERGOOD joined for duty. 2/Lieg. CUMMING joined for one month in lemur.	
			Very heavy snow storm in afternoon completely wrecked airline between BRETENCOURT and BLAIRVILLE and severely damaged the portion forward of the cutts place. 20 or 30 poles broken down. Everyone employed in rebuilding airline	
	3rd		do	do H/ALLEN T. hospital
	4th		do	do
	5th		do	do also lines to division on
	6		left laid also line between our left 21st H.Div and right Bde (167) of 56 H.Div.	

WAR DIARY or INTELLIGENCE SUMMARY

Army Form C. 2118

Sheet II

Place	Date	Hour	Summary of Events and Information	Remarks and references to Appendices
	April 7th		Completing lines and offices at BLAIRVILLE QUARRY	
	8th	3 pm	Advanced Divisional Headquarters opened at BLAIRVILLE QUARRY. Q Branch, ADMS, DADOS, remain at BRETENCOURT. Two orderly Offices kept open.	A (orders for opening of Offices) Plan No 1
BLAIRVILLE	9th		Boches attacking all day. Lines held good.	
	10th		Further fighting. Lt ALLEN returned to duty; Lt BAKER having done duty with RFA during his absence.	
		2 pm	ONT cable wagon proceeded to Brethyn Railway cutting and laid line from Pt Hypo in M 3.5 D to HENIN SUR COJEUL (a renewed) 90 Horse. Here 8 three good available cables were put to by a construction party from army while finishing afternoon route. Line to Colonel Irwin: gave trouble. One to 21 Div although not on maintenance was repaired to on Review close to their office. GSO1 expressed satisfaction at working 15 pairs. Dinner pressed into Corps reserve. Sup. 3.3 when in evidence with view to Kulcing me. Geo	

Army Form C. 2118

Sheet VII

WAR DIARY
or
INTELLIGENCE SUMMARY
(Erase heading not required.)

Place	Date	Hour	Summary of Events and Information	Remarks and references to Appendices
	April 12th	10.30am	Reconnaissance to Tpk at POMMIER by 4 pm.	
		1.70pm	Office at BRETENCOURT closed and instruments/personnel proceeded to POMMIER. Came under 18 Korps again.	
		5 pm	BLAIRVILLE exchange taken over late & the over. Changing Sigs 33 Div arrived POMMIER from Northern theo & theirs over took 30 minutes. Line at POMMIER from Nolue theo & theirs. No 3 cable wagon with detachment left with RA HQrs at BLAIRVILLE during operation 8th to 12th all this held good and line forward I mile although only cable line in the ground in trouble No observed. Visual station were manned but not used nor were under nets in power buzzers. Pigeons were ready but not present. Putting lines through to BOSSEUX (89 Bde) and SOUASTRE (90 Bde) in enemy route.	
POMMIER	13	10am	resting, clearing up lines & office	
	14		to	
	15		89 Bde moves to COUIN line arranged through PAS tent office	
	16		Div resting.	
	17			
	18		Received orders to take over from 5b Div Signals AGNY relachment	

Army Form C. 2118

WAR DIARY
or
INTELLIGENCE SUMMARY
(Erase heading not required.)

Sheet IV

Place	Date	Hour	Summary of Events and Information	Remarks and references to Appendices
POMMIER	APRIL 19th	3 pm	Div. H.Q. at POMMIER closed and opened at AGNY M.3.c. at same hour. Signal Office in very deep dugout with 12 inches of water on floor. 90 Bde moved in line with 21 Bde in support. 89 Bde moved to POMMIER. Line to first two Bdes fair but situation not very clear. Considerable number of buzzers stationed in test points along the lines at BEAURAINS, NEUVILLE VITASSE etc.	
AGNY		8.45 pm	Signal Office on fire. No casualties but all the lines from the Corps test dugout G front, also messages, registers and personal property of Signal Office staff. Fire was got under in about 30 minutes with considerable difficulty owing to dense smoke; box respirators were used by men entering one after another with good results. The cause of the fire is not clear, but as one drum of paraffin, 3rd full and a quantity of petrol was found, it is thought that the oil spectral must have been floating on the water. No instruments were damaged beyond local repair. New lines were him and communication reestablished to front brigades in about one hour and to the Corps in about 1½ hours. All the staff and buzzers worked very well all night clearing up.	
	20th		Clearing up remains of fire in Signal Office and improving lines generally. Lines found in bad condition with labelling very poor, some lines having labels with a different number on opposite sides of label. 89 H Bde moved into ACHICOURT MILL	

WAR DIARY or INTELLIGENCE SUMMARY

Army Form C. 2118

Sheet I

Place	Date	Hour	Summary of Events and Information	Remarks and references to Appendices
AGNY	APRIL 21		Signal office removed from down in dugouts and put in a new shelter above ground. Dugouts being gradually flooded out in spite of continual pumping. Change over was made by bringing up two new pair cables direct from Corps test point. Very little trouble was met in changing over. Ozenide detachment laid pair D5 cable from DON Hqrs near HENINEL to front M18 d 4.8 another detachment pair D5 cable from M18 d 4.8 to advanced 50 H Qrs GC102 to BEAURAINS test point. This was in preparation for opening of Divn: advanced H.Q. to establish (M18 d 4.3) in the meantime GC101 and 102 were put through and at BEAURAINS GC102 put through GRB4 to G test point and hence to YC2 giving another pair direct to DON. All available linesmen out improving lines to front Brigades. Line still bad and not at all clear. Visual station at BEAURAINS working to NEUVILLE VITASSE tested. Local circuits completed. Line laid by 89th Brigade men from DON exchange post HENINEL into support trenches of old HINDENBURG LINE to CAPT. BROCKHOLES, G.S.O.3 d/f front in N35c for a Divnl. O.P. Relay post Q is mounted near North Irish Horse established at NEUVILLE VITASSE: 20 the mounted men kept at this H.Q. Ronn [?] for motor cyclists. Capt. HINDLE is best in belief, such were the arrivals.	
	22			

WAR DIARY
or
INTELLIGENCE SUMMARY
(Erase heading not required.)

Army Form C. 2118

Sheet VI

Place	Date	Hour	Summary of Events and Information	Remarks and references to Appendices
AGNY	APRIL 23		90th Bde attacked at dawn. Lines working only fairly well, being occasionally cut by shell fire. Lines still difficult to trace across country. Overall detachment proceed to forward Divnl H.Q to lay in line from Kent point. 21 Bde proceeded later in day to support 90th Bde and afterwards also moved up; at one time all three Brigade Headquarters were at MENINEL. 90th Bde afternoon returned to NEUVILLE VITASSE. Lines held fairly well all day occasionally being cut by shell fire. Ymual was not needed but kept touch all through. Pigeons were not used on one or two occasions. On average time 7.35 am reached the tops at SIMENCO URT at 8 am. Wireless and power buzzers were not needed.	
	24th		Lines again straightened up but labelling in Brigade offices still not clear. Line being cut in and offices prepared for Advanced Divnl HQ M 18 d + 6.	
	25th		Advanced Divnl Headquarters opened at near NEUVILLE VITASSE. Working direct to 7thCorps, 30 DIV, 33 DIV and three Brigades; also back to AGNY exposed office YC2, which was kept opened for traffic for Q, ADMS etc. Still working in lines both back and forward.	APPENDIX "B"

Army Form C. 2118

Sheet VII

WAR DIARY
or
INTELLIGENCE SUMMARY
(Erase heading not required.)

Instructions regarding War Diaries and Intelligence Summaries are contained in F.S. Regs., Part II. and the Staff Manual respectively. Title Pages. will be prepared in manuscript.

Place	Date	Hour	Summary of Events and Information	Remarks and references to Appendices
NEUVILLE-VITASSE M18d4.2	April 26th		Improving lines. Visual station moved forward to enter end of NEUVILLE VITASSE village. Good signals from there to new Brigade Hdqrs n neatridge	
	27th		Working on lines: also recovered GC102 back from Y22R & BEAURAINS. Also lines being picked up in AGNY by party from Y.C.2. Divn command of 18th Signal Coy came over to Coytown.	
	28th	8am	Signal office at Y.C.2 closed and Office relief proceeded under Captain HINDLE to ROLLECOURT near ST. POL to open new signal office there. Sig 18th Divn thieven go over lines forward and Littlework and at rear fronts. Instrument of 18th Signals being installed.	
	29th	12 noon	Cable wagons and transport at AGNY proceeded by road to ROLLECOURT. Office at NEUVILLE VITASSE handed over to 18th Divn Signals. Whole company arrived at ROLLECOURT. Communication established through 3rd Army office to 19th Corps at FLERS, also to 89 Bde at NUNCQ and 90 Bde at CROIX. 21st Bde moving into BUNEVILLE.	
	30th	11:30am	Communication to 21st Bde established by direct cable line. Office being cleaned up. Local circuits completed.	

PLAN N° 1

Railway Cutting

DRAFT PLAN OF LINES
- ┼┼┼┼┼ 6 wire D pair airline
- ─────── Buried cable
- ─ ─ ─ ─ D5 twisted
- ─ · ─ · ─ 4 pair airline
- · · · · · · D5 single

Instruments
21 Bde Sc + phone
  on ~~GR5~~ YC23
  and phone on
  GR 1 forward

90 Bde exchange
  on GR 3
  and D3 on GR 14

89 Bde Sc + phone
  on GR 8
  and phone on
  GR 5 forward

RA take
  GR 2·4·6 forward
  and GR 7

GR 11
to ADV S. DIV
(our maintenance)

Instruments
Sc YC2 & YC2R
  on GR 1
Exchange YC2 & YC2R
  on GR 4 and GR 10
Direct YC2R to Corps
  or exchange
  on GR 3
Direct RA to Corps
  on GR 2

FICHEUX

GR 7
GR 8
GR 2·4·6
GR 1·3·5
Corps YC23
GR 17
GR 9
G. STAFF
BLAIRVILLE QUARRY
note 4 D3 on Two Circuits
DROP
Div H.Q.
T STA
GR 16
RA
YC2R
GR 18
No 7
To 21 DIV (their maintenance)
GR 15
GR 16
B.AUMONT DUG OUT
YC2
BRETENCOURT

NOTES GR18 to Labellea
RB airline D5 twisted to lay from from YC2 & YC2R on 12 line write to the further front
2·16 in being laid by Army Signal Coy
17 do do do
APM but will have to Labellea
G 15 to Labellea
YC2 & YC2R at exchange
GR 7 & GR 15

30TH DIVISIONAL SIGNAL COMPANY – ROYAL ENGINEERS.

"A"

The Advanced Divisional H.Q. (Y.C.Z.R) will open at BLAIRVILLE QUARRY at 3 p.m. to-morrow, 8th instant.

The following will be the distribution of personnel:—

OFFICERS.	Captain Hindle.	YCZR I/c lines & linemen. Wagon.
	2/Lieut. Baker.	YCZR at R.A & available for Cable
	2/Lieut. Cummins	YCZR i/c visual and camp.
	2/Lieut. Scattergood.	YCZ i/c.

SIGNAL OFFICE STAFF.
    Corporal Ince i/c.
  Sapper Mc.Gregor. Sapper Heath.
   " Martin.   " Crosby.
   " Griffiths.   " Gregory.
   " Percy.   " Roskell.
   " Kelly.   Pioneer Rouffignac.
    Pioneer Munn. *Spr Barnett*

ORDERLIES. Private Pritchard. Private Jaycock.
      " Healey.   " Boudin.
        Private Humphries.

CHECKS. Driver Robinson. Driver Tinwell.

LINEMEN.
    Sergt. Ferridge i/c.
    L/Cpl. Lewthwaite (indoor lineman)
    Spr. Colley.
     " Wharton.
     " Clays.
     " Ogden (on instruments)

CABLE WAGON. No. 1 Cable Wagon and limber will be at Y.C.Z.R. complete with all stores and equipment, and must always be ready to move at 20 minutes notice.
    Corporal Mc.Ewan i/c.
  Sapper Watson. Sapper Paxton.
   " Jones.   " Rogers.
   " Richardson.   " Smith.
   " Stockton
    and Drivers.

Mules and 4 Riding Horses.

Working numbers to be arranged by N.C.O. i/c.

Any lineman of the above detachment may be called upon for lineman's duties if considered necessary by the N.C.O. i/c Linemen.

LIGHTING LORRY. The Lighting Lorry will proceed as early as possible to Advanced Headquarters, BLAIRVILLE QUARRY, and fit up Offices etc.

RATIONS. L/Cpl. Hartnoll will be in charge of rations and the issuing. All rations for the party at Y.C.Z.R. must be dumped at BLAIRVILLE QUARRY by noon of day of opening Y.C.Z.R. This will include rations for Z to Z+3 days.

WATER. Water can be obtained in BLAIRVILLE and will have to be carried in tins from there. Tins will have to be taken.

MOVEMENTS. No. 1 Cable Wagon and Signal Office staff will parade at 10 a.m. and proceed direct to BLAIRVILLE QUARRY reporting on arrival to 2/Lieut. Cummins. Corporal Ince will arrange to have the office ready for traffic at 2-30 p.m.

Y.C.Z. All N.C.O's and men not mentioned above will remain at BRETENCOURT.

The following, with No. 3 Cable Wagon, will be the detachment standing by at one hour's notice:-

                Sergt. Morton i/c.
Sapper Lashbrook.   Pioneer Burrow.
Pnr. Harrison.   "   Naylor.
         Pnr. Shaw.
Also available, if necessary, Sapper Dale.

Drivers of No. 3 Wagon.

OFFICE STAFF.
(Y.C.Z) The Office at BRETENCOURT will remain open with the following staff:-

2/Cpl. Heal.   L/Cpl. Shaw.
Spr. Bennett.   Spr. Belcher.
"   Atkinson.   "   Fielding.
"   Heal.   "   Hakes.
Pnr. Fenton.   Pnr. McLaren.
      Pte. Thompson.

LINEMEN.(Y.C.Z)   Sapper Keeling.
                   "   Davidson.
             Corps Lineman.

MOTOR CYCLIST
D.R's. Corporal Forsey.   Corporal Horsfall.
        "   Jaffrey.   "   Kerr.
        "   Rollinson.   "   Garlick.

MOUNTED D.R's. Privates Wilson and Wills.

2/Lieut. Scattergood will arrange duties.

[signature]

Captain, R.E.
O.C., 30TH DIVISIONAL SIGNAL COY. R.E.

IN THE FIELD,
7th April, 1917.

COOKS.	L/Cpl. Washington with Sapper Richardson will cook for Headquarters and No. 1 Cable Wagon, but the latter will be available for cable detachment when it moves.
BATMAN.	Privates Baynes and Kirchin and Driver White A. will be with Y.C.Z.R. Duties from 2/Lieut. Baker.
GROOMS.	Drivers Scott and Bevan, with four Chargers will be at Y.C.Z.R.
VISUAL PARTY.	The visual men as below will come under 2/Lieut. Cummins for orders. They have proceeded direct to the Station and will man it by 3 p.m. on the 8th inst.

                L/Corpl. Burrows i/c.
Private Twiggs.   Private Greatorex.
    "   Nickle.   " McBride.
    "   Clay.   " Watson.

MOUNTED D.R's.	Corporal Rutherford. Private Soper. Private Hope. **Private Dewar.** will be available for D.R. runs of a non-urgent nature. Also for carrying prisoners documents from the Divisional Collecting Station to Corps Collecting Cage at BERNEVILLE. Duties to be arranged by Corporal Ince. There must always be one ready to move off.
INSTRUMENTS.	Sapper Dale will arrange to collect telephones from G.O.C., G.S.O. I, and G.R.E. after 11 a.m. and proceed with limber wagon to Y.C.Z.R. and re-fit phones there, afterwards returning to Y.C.Z.
LINEMEN AT BDES.	Corporal Willson with Sappers Duthoit, Exton, and Blackmore will proceed at 9 a.m. to 21st Brigade in the railway cutting and report to the Signal Officer for duty as linemen on back lines and lateral to Brigade of the 56th Division (G.R.12 line). They will take 2 horses, kits, and rations up to Z 3 day. Instructions will be issued later as to patrolling of lines.
MOUNTED D.R's AT BRIGADES.	Privates Nicholson and Gray will proceed to 89th Brigade Headquarters and report to the Signal Officer for duty, rationed up to Z+3 day. Rations will be taken with Corporal Willson's wagon.

MOTOR CYCLIST D.R's.	Sergt. Ashley i/c
	Corporal Bradshaw. Corporal Clough.
	      Cook. Roughly.
	      Corpl. Nuttall.
	will be at Y.C.Z.R. Sergt. Ashley to arrange runs.
	Motor Cyclist D.R's are to be saved as much as possible for special runs.

CAMP.	2/Lieut. Cummins will be in charge of the camp and will detail billets, cookhouses, horse lines, and latrines. The various dugouts and tents will be numbered and no man is to change his billet without special permission. A list of men, with numbers of their billets will be placed in the Signal Office. All Orderlies and checks are to know where every billet is.
MOVEMENTS.	

30TH DIVISIONAL SIGNAL COMPANY, R.E.

"B"

Advanced Divisional H.Q. will open at M.18.d.4.2.6 to-morrow, the 25th instant, at 11 a.m.

Signal Office at AGNY will remain open for "Q", A.D.M.S., A.P.M., D.A.D.O.S., S.S.O., etc.

Circuits at Y.C.Z. will be:-

Baseboard superimposed to G.C.O.
S.C. Set   "   to Y.C.Z.R.
10-line ringing exchange with:-
    G.C.O.
    Y.C.Z. 1.
    Y.C.Z. 2.
    50th Division.
    "Q"
    (D.A.D.O.S.
    (S.S.O.
Buzzer unit with:-
    A.P.M.
    A.D.M.S.
    Signals Mess.
    Local.

Circuits at Y.C.Z.R. will be:-

Single current set superimposed to G.C.O.
   "   "   "   "   "   to Y.C.Z.

Buzzer working to
    89th Brigade.
    21st Brigade.
    90th Brigade.
10-line exchange with
    G.O.C.
    G.S.O. 1.
    "G"
    "A"
    C.R.E.
    R.A.
    33rd Division later 21st Division.
    50th Division Adv. later the 14th Division.
    Y.C.Z. 1.
    Y.C.Z. 2.

ii Lieut. SCATTERGOOD with Corporal INCE will take up complete full relief to man Y.C.Z.R., taking Orderlies and the following linemen:-
    Sergt. FERRIDGE.
    Sapper COLLEY.

Lorry will take party less those on bicycles and will leave at 8 a.m. taking all kits, etc., Office stationary, and two tables for D.R.L.S. etc.

Corporal INCE will detail reliefs to man Y.C.Z.

Sergt. ASHLEY will detail four Motor Cyclists to proceed to Y.C.Z.R. to report on arrival at 10 a.m. to ii Lieut. SCATTERGOOD. The remainder of the M.C. D.R's, less two now with "Q", will proceed to Y.C.Z.R. after "G" Staff leaves Y.C.Z. i.e. 11 a.m.

Two Horse D.R's will remain at Y.C.Z., other D.R's as at present.

Artificer will remain at Y.C.Z.

ii Lieut. SCATTERGOOD will arrange to join up instruments and test by 6-30 a.m. and then stand by. The four Wall Telephones in Instrument Stores will go with the first party on lorry.

(1)

Corporal MCEWAN and detachment will remain at Y.C.Z.R.

C.S.M. will detail a party under 2/Cpl. HARRIS to load Officers' Kits and dismantle the four tents near the Signal Office. All to be ready to go in G.S. Wagon to Y.C.Z.R. by 10 a.m. Loading party will proceed with wagon and unload and put up tents.

ii Lieut. BAKER will proceed to Y.C.Z.R. with Advanced Party and complete arrangements of leading in of cables. On complete establishment of Y.C.Z.R. Office he will proceed with two linemen and patrol lines forward, paying special attention to correct labelling of lines especially in NEUVILLE VITASSE and HENINEL Offices.

Lorry on unloading at Y.C.Z.R. will return to Y.C.Z. and load up at Officers Mess and return to Y.C.Z.R. for further orders.

Lighting Lorry will dismantle circuits at daylight and proceed to Y.C.Z.R. and put up lights in huts.

Captain HINDLE will remain in charge of Y.C.Z. from 8 a.m. onwards.

ii Lieutl CUMMING will arrange camp at Y.C.Z.R. and afterwards be prepared to move visual station forward to NEUVILLE VITASSE where a 'phone circuit to latter place from Y.C.Z.R. has been arranged.

Corporal WINSTANLEY with party, with feeds and rations, will proceed to test box on F X Route about 200 yards N.W. of AGNY-WAILLY ROAD and will pick up double D.5 Cable line G.R. 11 from there to BLAIRVILLE QUARRY returning to Y.C.Z. and reporting exact amount of cable recovered. Line is on trees and as many ladders as possible will be taken with the cable wagon.

C.Q.M.S. Stores, Instrument Repairer, and Company Office will remain at AGNY for the present.

Chargers for O.C., ii Lieut. BAKER, and ii Lieut. CUMMING will proceed to Y.C.Z.R.

CAPTAIN R.E.
O.C., 300TH DIVISIONAL SIGNAL COY.R.E.

IN THE FIELD,
24-4-17.

Corporal MORGAN and detachment will remain at Y.O.S.R.

O.C.M will detail a party under 2/Cpl. BAILIE to load Grierson, hits and dismantle the four tents near the Signal Office, and to be ready to go in G.S. Wagon to Y.O.S.R. by 10 a.m. Loading party will proceed with wagon and unload and put up tents.

Ilchiest. RAIN will proceed to Y.O.S.R. with Advanced Party and complete arrangements of loading in of cables. On complete establishment of Y.O.S.R. Office he will proceed with two linesmen and patrol lines forward, paying special attention to correct labelling of lines especially in INDIVIDUAL VILLAGE and FAMINE cables.

Lorry on unloading at Y.O.S.R. will return to M.O.R. and load up at Office and proceed and return to Y.O.S.R. for further orders.

Lighting Lorry will dismantle circuits at daylight and proceed to Y.O.S.R. M.M. and pick up lights in huts.

Corpls. HINDLE will remain in charge of Y.O.R. from 8 a.m. onwards.

Lt M'NEIL QUARING will arrange camp at Y.O.S.R. and afterwards be prepared to move visual station forward to INDIVIDUAL VILLAGE where a 'phone circuit to latter place from Y.O.S.R. has been arranged.

Corporal VINCATERLIN with party, with feeds and rations will proceed to task box on P.K Route about 600 yards N.E. of ARMY-DAIRY ROAD and will pick up Cable D.8 Cable line G.R. 11 from there to BATTALION HEAD returning to Y.O.S.R. and reporting cable amount of cable recovered. This is an area where enemy battens on passable will be taken with the cable wagon.

O.C.M.B. Stores, Instrument keepers, and Company Clerks will remain at ARMY for the present.

Chargemen for O.C., Lt Black, C.S.M., and Lt Stant. CURRING will proceed to Y.O.S.R.

IN THE FIELD
24-8-17

J. O'O., 39TH DIVISION, SIGNAL COY.R.S.
CAPTAIN R.E.

30TH Divisional Signal Coy

May 1917

Vol 19

Map No 2 is dated 16/5/19

But Sheet III refers to it.

Hence date is probably
16/5/17

Secret.

Vol 19

WAR DIARY
OF THE
30TH DIVISIONAL SIGNAL COMPANY, ROYAL ENGINEERS
FOR
MAY, 1917.
VOLUME XLX.

[signature] Major,
30th Divisional Signal Coy.
R.E.

WAR DIARY
INTELLIGENCE SUMMARY

Army Form C. 2118.

Sheet 1

Place	Date	Hour	Summary of Events and Information	Remarks and references to Appendices
ROELLECOURT	May 1st			
	2nd		Cable wagons overhauled, stores sorted out. Light reinforcements sent as cable drums tested in cable laying. Brigade on wind. Received instructions for move of Divnl. HQrs. to OEUF. Div Cable wagons under 2/Lt BAKER proceeded to OEUF ready to lay lines to Brigades. 19th Corps building line from FLERS to OEUF. Following lines laid. TR 2 from 2nd Bde at BLANGERMONT to OEUF.	
	3rd		by detachment under 2/Lt CUMMING. TR1 from OEUF to FONTAINE D'ETALON to 90th Bde and SF1 and 2A from a Corps airline FF1 and 2 running from FLERS through VILLERS line being tees on at telephone: working to 89th Bde: at NOEUX. Line from Corps finished. Lines were strong up to good, time except 90th Bde line: very weak signals for sometime. Local circuit 89 & Divn. G Office at the enemy village. Company marched to OEUF.	
OEUF		3pm	Signal Office at OEUF opened: ROELLECOURT closed down. Wagons at 89th and 90th Brigades reeled out.	

War Diary.

No 1.

30th DIVISION
COMMUNICATIONS
4-5-17

Map – Lens 11
Scale 1:10000

CABLE ————————
AIRLINE. —·—·—·—·—·—

Note:— The line from YCZ to permanent route Hesdin – St. Pol. Road laid when TCO moved from Flers to St Pol. on 18.5.17.

(Locations shown on map: Humieres, To St Pol, Permanent Route, To Aesdin, YCZ, OEJ, Villeman, TRI, Fontaine l'Etalon, ZIZ, ST, Eclagnemont ZU, TCO, Flers, TCO to St Pol 12.10.5.17, Kinchel, Baubers, Boffles, Noeux, Villers, ZHI)

WAR DIARY
or
INTELLIGENCE SUMMARY.

(Erase heading not required.)

Army Form

Sheet II

Instructions regarding War Diaries and Intelligence Summaries are contained in F.S. Regs., Part II. and the Staff Manual respectively. Title pages will be prepared in manuscript.

Place	Date	Hour	Summary of Events and Information	Remarks, references to Appendices
OEUF	May 4th		Local lines in village completed and main lines patrolled. Cable detachments returned from Brigades and rejoined company. Class for twenty battalion signallers commenced. Instruction in buzzer work, visual etc. 1 O.R. joined today.	MAP N°1
	5th		Corps WOOTON. Lines patrolled. Brigades out on visual schemes. Class for linemen under Sergt Jennings started. WOD or reinforcements under training for cable work and airline.	
	6th		Training continued. 2 Lt HEPBURN and THOMPSON proceeded on 48 hours leave to PARIS.	
	7th		Training continued. 2nd Lt N.E. BAKER left for duty with Heavy Branch M.G.C. Machine Gun Corps.	
	8th		Training. Visual class continued.	
	9th		do	
	10th		do New line laid from OEUF to HUMIERES to join permanent route HESDIN – ST POL ready for move of 19th Corps H.Q.	
	11th		Training. Line to HUMIERES completed.	
	12th		do 19th Corps moved to ST. POL. Working on new line. OC'd line to FLERS	

New diary

30th DIVISION
COMMUNICATIONS

N° 2

MAP LENS II
1:100000

Hesdin.

TCO
St-Pol.

Willeman
Wail
Fontaine-l'Étalon
Queux
Vaulx

Army Form C. 2118.

WAR DIARY
or
INTELLIGENCE SUMMARY.
(Erase heading not required.)

SHEET No. 111

Place	Date	Hour	Summary of Events and Information	Remarks and references to Appendices
OEUF	12th July		Put through to line FF1+2 to 89th Bde at NOEUX and to AUXI-LE-CHATEAU.	
	13th		Drawing - Capt W.R. ALLEN, R.A. Signals, returned from leave to England and rejoined R.A. Hedqrs at ACHICOURT.	
	14th		Drawing - Preparing for move of Division to WILLEMAN and moving of 21st Bde to WAIL and 89th Bde to VAULX. Line laid from 90th Bde office to VAULX.	
	15th		Packing up and moving to WILLEMAN. Lines taken over have been 1st Cavalry Division. Line TR1 OEUF to FONTAINE and WILLEMAN and laid forward to 90th Bde and extension to 1/1st Surrey Lancs Regt at OEUF.	
WILLEMAN	16th	2am	Opened Signal office at WILLEMAN	Map No 2
	17th		Lines patrolled and training continued	
	18th		do	
	19th		do	
			Preparing to move. Cable detachments No 2 and 3 proceeded to 89th and 90th. The Bdgrs ready to pick up line on 20th inst.	

WAR DIARY or INTELLIGENCE SUMMARY.

Army Form C. 2118.

Sheet IV

Place	Date May	Hour	Summary of Events and Information	Remarks and references to Appendices
WILLEMAN	20th		No 1 detachment picked up (part) TRI line up as WAIL and also D3 line from 21st Bd HQ to 4C2. No 2 detachment picked up TR3 L/103 detachment TRI. Local lines recovered. All three poles moved 21st to CRDIX, 89 & 5 NUNC & 90 to BLANGERMONT. No new lines laid to Bde. DR service only. Advance party of 15th Div Signals arrived. Instruments changed	
	21st	10 am	Signal Office handed over to 75th DIV. Company proceeded by route march to PERNES.	
PERNES		12 noon	Office at PERNES opened. Only circuit to PERNES exchange and thence to 1st Army. G + Q phones fitted only. DR service to Brigades which moved to, 21st Bde EQUIRRE, 89th - ANTIGNEU CHT. 90th - SACHIN	
NORRENT FONTES	22nd	10 am	Hd Qtrs moved to NORRENT FONTES. Working third summer rod phone to 1st ARMY and same to 21st Bde at LAIRES through army lines. Maurice only to Bde of ST. HILAIRE. And 90th Bde at FONTAINE.	

WAR DIARY
or
INTELLIGENCE SUMMARY.
(Erase heading not required.)

Army Form C. 2118.

Sheet No. V

Place	Date	Hour	Summary of Events and Information	Remarks and references to Appendices
MORBENT FONTES	May 23		Resting and overhauling wagons. R.E. and gunners inspected.	
STEENBECQUE	24	10 am	Opened signal office at STEENBECQUE. Direct wire to 2nd Army. Telephone closed MORBENT FONTES same hour.	
CAESTRE	25	10 am	Opened signal office CAESTRE. Direct wire to 2nd Corps and phones to 93rd Bn. Hvy Arty and 21st Bde. BRO. V.C.K.	
	26	10 am	Closed STEENBECQUE. Opened signal office WATOU. Direct wire to 2nd Corps and 21st Bde. and through Corps to 90th Bde	
WATOU	27		Resting. Advance party of eight linesmen left for 24th Div Hd BRANDHOEK. Eight drivers and cable hands arrived.	
	28		Division resting	
	29		do do	
	30	9 am	R. Arty rejoined Division. Signal office closed WATOU. Took over from 24th Div. at BRANDHOEK. 89th Bde in front line - 21st Bde in support - BRANDHOEK. 90th Bde in reserve in heat	
BRANDHOEK	31		Settling in at BRANDHOEK. 90th Bde moving back to training area	

30 Divisional Signal Coy

June 1917

Vol 20

SECRET.

WAR DIARY
OF THE
30TH DIVISIONAL SIGNAL COMPANY, R.E.
FOR
JUNE 1917.

VOLUME XX.

5-7-17.

[signature] Major, R.E.

Vol 20

Army Form C. 2118.

WAR DIARY
or
INTELLIGENCE SUMMARY.
(Erase heading not required.)

Sheet I

Place	Date 1917	Hour	Summary of Events and Information	Remarks and references to Appendices
BRANDHOEK	1st		Establishing lines and wireless communications generally	
	2nd		do do do Corps Wireless station near Dumel Hgrs working to station at Bde Hdqrs in the transport's YPRES. Bde also working forward from Bde Hqrs to Battalion at Dormy House. Power Buzzers established in both right and left companies of each battalion working to Bn Hqrs at Battalion Hqrs (at Dormy House and HALFWAY House.	MAP Belgium Sht 28 NW Sh 5A
	3rd		Lines in rising and lowering work continued & reinforcements maintained. L/Corp proceeded to GHQ wireless corp. L/Cp WRIGHT 2nd R.S.F. acting as Bde Signal Officer.	
	4th		do do	
	5th			
	6th		Lines in buried system broken by shelling, heavy work in repairing under Area Officer I/c buried system and good work in repairing being accomplished by Lieut. Purdy and L/Cpls BEAN's, Spr EXTON, DAVIDSON and Pte DINGWALL	

A5834 Wt.W4973 M687 750,000 8/16 D. D. & L. Ltd. Forms/C.2118/13.

Army Form C. 2118.

WAR DIARY
or
INTELLIGENCE SUMMARY.
(Erase heading not required.)

Sheet II

Place	Date	Hour	Summary of Events and Information	Remarks and references to Appendices
BRANDHOEK (contd)	7th		2/Lt H.E.M. SWAN joined for duty and posted to command Nos 1, 2, & 3 cable detachments.	
	8th		Hunting lines. Big attack today. Lines all worked well.	
	9th		do	
	10th		do Commenced making new forward cable routes. Left HindH.E.m charge with assistance of Corps Signals Office.	
	11th		As above	
	12th/13		do do New normal roll for HQ, RAHQ, NOTs entrained. Advanced party proceeded ahead to RENINGHELST.	APPENDIX "A"
RENINGHELST	14th	11a	Offices opened. Considerable difficulty with lines both back and front owing to 10th Corps tel. division, at H.4.41.a-not getting off our routes as arranged.	

Army Form C. 2118.

WAR DIARY
or
INTELLIGENCE SUMMARY.
(Erase heading not required.)

Sheet 111

Instructions regarding War Diaries and Intelligence Summaries are contained in F. S. Regs., Part II. and the Staff Manual respectively. Title pages will be prepared in manuscript.

Place	Date	Hour	Summary of Events and Information	Remarks and references to Appendices
RENINGHELST	15th		Settling in and establishing various local lines. (Lt Col GOWAN rejoined section from G.H.Q. Wireless Course)	
	16th		do	
	17th		Commenced burying cables in forward areas from existing battalion Hqrs near DORMY HOUSE towards front line. Working parties provided by infantry supervised by Signal Officer provided by Corps under general direction of Captain HINDLE.	
	18		Buried work continued do	
	19		do	
	20		do Route on south side of ZILLEBEKE started	
	21		do	
	22		do	
	23		do Major HOWORTH leave to England	
	24		do	
	25		do Lt McGOWAN admitted hospital (sick)	
	26		do	

WAR DIARY
INTELLIGENCE SUMMARY.

Army Form C. 2118.

Sheet IV

Place	Date	Hour	Summary of Events and Information	Remarks and references to Appendices
REMINGHELST	25th		Buried routes continued	
	26		do new route BEDFORD HOUSE to YEOMANRY Post. 2/88 Brigade, 1st 2 Bn. King's Liverpool Regt (since taken over by Canadian Divn 3rd Infantry)	
	29th		do new route RUDKIN HOUSE to EQ 4 Support line	
	30		do Captain HINDLE proceeded to ENGLAND	

Considerable difficulty experienced in keeping up existing communication especially during period 23rd-30th owing to intense shelling. Shelling the buried lines in some cases the Start Points being blown in & destroyed.
All crews during this time very hard worked both on maintenance and in new work.

30TH DIVISION COMMUNICATIONS.
30-5-17

REFERENCE
Air Line ————
Railed Cable –○–○–○–
Buried Cable ————

30 Divisional Signal Coy

July 1917

Vol 21

Secret.

Vol 21

WAR DIARY

of the

30TH DIVISIONAL SIGNAL COMPANY, R.E.

for the
month of

JULY, 1917.

VOLUME XXI.

[signature], Major, R.E.

1st August, 1917.

Appendix A.

30TH DIVISIONAL SIGNAL COMPANY – ROYAL ENGINEERS.

NOMINAL ROLL OF HEADQUARTERS & NO. 1 SECTIONS.

C.S.M.:-

    Marcham   R.C.M.

C.Q.M.S.:-

    Kellar   W.B.

Sergeants:-

Ashley	H.E.	M.C.D.R.
Ferridge	E.V.	
Haworth	A.	
May	W.J.	O.T.

Corporals:-

(A/Sergt.)	Barnett	C.	S. & C.S.
(do.)	Morton	W.	C.W.Commander.
	Inee	H.	Supt. Signal Office.
	Mc.Ewan	W.	C.W.Commander.
	Willson	H.	i/c R.A.Hq.Sig.Staff.
	Winstanley	J.T.	C.W.Commander.
	Wootton	T.	do.

M.C.D.R's:-

Bradshaw	H.I.	
Clough	A.S.	
Cook	J.M.	
Ferguson	D.C.	
Forsey	A.G.	
Garlick	W.H.	Artificer.
Horsfall	A.	
Jaffrey	H.	
Jennings	G.	
Kerr	J.M.	
Ledson	J.H.	
Nuttall	H.	
Rollinson	F.	
Roughley	H.	
Williams	C.G.	

2nd Corporals:-

(A/Cpl)	Higson	A.J.	P.E.L.Corpl.
	Harris	C.F.	Pay Corporal.
	Keys	F.W.	

Lance-Corporals:-

(A/2/Cpl.)	Lewthwaite	W.	
	Washington	W.	Cook.
(Unpaid)	Hartnoll	H.	

Office Telegraphists:-

L/Cpl)			
A/2/Cpl.)	Shaw	J.	Signalmaster.
A/2/Cpl.	Mc.Gregor	J.M.	do.
A/L/Cpl.	Heath	W.F.	do.

Sappers:-	Atkinson	R.
	Barnett	A.H.
	Bayliss	T.
	Belcher	F.
	Bennett	G.W.
	Blake	H.
	Cameron	W.F.
	Crosby	C.
	Craik	T.
	Dawson	W.
	Fielding	J.
	Gregory	T.W.
	Griffiths	T.G.
	Heal	O.W.
	Henry	E.
	Kelly	T.
	Martin	W.
	Molyneux	A.
	Noel	F.
	Percy	G.H.
	Roskell	W.E.
	Stanton	J.K.

Sappers other than O.T's:-

(A/L/Cpl.)	Clays	E.	Cableman
(do.)	Colley	C.	do.
(do.)	Wharton	J.	do.
(do.)			
unpaid.	Rogers	A.	do.
	Appleyard	W.	do.
	Blackmore	H.	do.
	~~Brown~~	~~W.~~	~~do.~~
	Butler	W.B.	
	~~Conibere~~	~~W.~~	~~Cableman~~
	Dale	H.	Instrument repairer.
	Davidson	T.	Cableman.
	Duthoit	W.	do.
	Dunn	W.R.	do.
	Exton	G.R.	do.
	Fenton	E.	Telephone Operator.
	Hague	A.	Cableman.
	Henham	E.	Saddler.
	Harrison	F.A.	Cableman.
	Jones	S.	do.
	Keeling	F.W.	do.

Sappers other than O.T's (contd):-

Lashbrook	F.W.	Wheelwright.
Munn	F.E.	Telephone Operator.
Mc.Kenzie	W.	Cableman.
Newham	H.M.	do.
Ogden	L.	Instrument repairer.
Paxton	T.	Wheelwright.
Pleavin	H.	Cableman.
Parrott	A.H.	do.
Richardson	P.	do.
Rouffignac	C.	Telephone Operator.
Smith	H.	Cableman.
Stockton	C.	do.
Swindells	P.	Saddler.
~~Sedgemore~~	~~T.J.~~	~~Cableman.~~
~~Simpson~~	~~J.~~	~~do.~~
~~Tate~~	~~G.H.~~	~~do.~~
Watson	J.R.	do.
Webster	W.	do.

Pioneers:-

Baker	W.W.	G.D.Pioneer.
~~Baker~~	~~A.E.~~	~~Cableman.~~
Ball	G.	G.D.Pioneer.
Burrows	A.	Cableman.
Burrows	R.	G.D.Pioneer.
~~Copeland~~	~~A.~~	~~Cableman.~~
Dingwall	N.	do.
~~Dickinson~~	~~J.G.~~	~~do.~~
Evans	W.	G.D.Pioneer.
Fitzsimmons	J.	do.
Hesketh	T.	Cableman.
Lewis	G.	G.D.Pioneer.
Mc.Laren	W.	Telephone Operator.
Marks	F.C.	G.D.Pioneer.
Naylor	F.	Cableman.
Rich	W.S.	G.D.Pioneer.
Shaw	J.	do.
Simpson	G.	do.
Thompson	J.G.	Telephone Operator.
Toft	S.	G.D.Pioneer.
Washbourne	H.	do.
Wyld	A.	

Drivers:-

Apperley	S.P.
Bailey	P.
Barrett	J.A.
Bevan	T.
Chaldecott	H.R.
Chapman	J.
England	F.
Fenton	J.A.
Fox	F.
Goodman	W.B.
Hardy	J.
Hetherington	J.
Heywood	P.
Ingle	R.H.
Jordan	J.H.
Jakes	A.
Marsh	R.
Nicholls	C.H.
Pack	C.
Plunkett	C.W.
Ramsbottom	E.
Robinson	V.
Rushton	R.
Rushworth	P.
Scott	J.
Smith	J.
Sheppard	J.B.
Thompson	W.
Vass	C.
Weddupp	W.
White	A.
White	S.N.
Woodworth	G.

A.S.C. Personnel:-

Amphlett	E.E.	30-cwt Lorry.
Bond	R.H.	P.E.L. Lorry.
Clark	W.	30-cwt Lorry.
Middleton	J.	Motor car driver.
Parlee	G.K.	P.E.L. Lorry.

R.F.A. Brigade Signal Sub-sections.

148 Brigade:-

    Corpl. (A/Sergt.) Newby   F.

    2/Cpl.   Clarkson   G.H.

Sapper A/L/Cpl.	Brind	T.
Sapper	Chadwick	G.
"	Dexter	A.G.
"	Kirton	C.M.

Pionr.	Anderson	G.
"	Ashman	W.
"	Flower	W.A.
"	Horrex	C.C.R.
"	Johnston	S.

Driver	Douglas	W.
"	Kirkham	J.H.

149 Brigade:-

    Corpl. A/Sgt.   Charlton   F.

    2/Cpl.   Riley   C.

Sapper	Baker	E.
"	Dellow	E.
"	Wadsworth	H.
"	Wallace	T.

Pionr.	Barton	A.
"	Greenhalgh	S.
"	Harrison	W.H.
"	Lorraine	G.B.S.
"	Perry	A.
"	Waters	W.R.

Driver	Rutt	H.
"	Hill	W.

Army Form C. 2113.

WAR DIARY
or
INTELLIGENCE SUMMARY.
(Erase heading not required.)

Sheet 1

Instructions regarding War Diaries and Intelligence Summaries are contained in F. S. Regs., Part II. and the Staff Manual respectively. Title pages will be prepared in manuscript.

Place	Date	Hour	Summary of Events and Information	Remarks and references to Appendices
RENINGHELST	1917 July 1st		Buried cable work continued. Heavy shelling and consequent damage to line	
	2nd		do	
	3rd		do	
	4th		Burnt do Major HOWORTH returned from leave	
	5th		do Lieut DALLISON joined for duty	
	6th		Buried cable work suspended during change of division. Silent period in forward area. No telephoning allowed. Wireless, power buzzers, visual & runners only used. Amm. Column Duty left RENINGHELST to NORDAUSQUE to prepare office. Cable wagons and transport proceeded by road return as WAEMARS-CAPPEL	
NORDAUSQUE	7th		Office closed at RENINGHELST and opened NORDAUSQUE 10 a.m	
	8th		Running lines to 90th Bde: and S.C.O. local circuits. 21st Bde, 8th Bde and 8 Corps thro' existing permanent lines.	
	9th		Linesmen resting. O.T.'s being trained in Wireless.	
	10		do	

A 5834 Wt. W4973/M687 750,000 8/16 D. D. & L. Ltd. Forms/C.2118/13.

Army Form C. 2118.

WAR DIARY
or
INTELLIGENCE SUMMARY.
(Erase heading not required.)

Sheet II

Instructions regarding War Diaries and Intelligence Summaries are contained in F. S. Regs., Part II. and the Staff Manual respectively. Title pages will be prepared in manuscript.

Place	Date	Hour	Summary of Events and Information	Remarks and references to Appendices
NORDAUSQUE	July 11th		Company resting: overhauling instruments. Car proceeded to DSC for overhaul.	
	12th		Resting	
	13th		Lt DALLISON with 12 Lieuren proceeded to forward area for work	
	14th		Lt SCATTERGOOD with 6 OTs proceeded to 8" Corps for one week's course in wireless. Divisional field day. Visual enemies only used.	
	15th		Lt SWAN with 12 Lieuren proceeded to forward area party.	
	16th		Lieuren infantry working here.	
	17th		Picking up lines in rearward	
	18th		do	
	19th		Officer closed NORDAUSQUE 10am reopened at STEENVORDE at same hour. Circuit to II Corps and 21st Div. do to Bre thro II corps.	
STEENVORDE	20th		Preparing = forward area.	
	21st		do 2 Lt. SWAN. M.E.M. to hospital.	
	22nd		do	
	23rd		do advance party to advanced H.Q.	accidentally injury Knee.
	24th		Officer closed STEENVORDE 10am opened advanced Div HQ. H27.b.6570 (Sheet 28)	

WAR DIARY or INTELLIGENCE SUMMARY

Army Form C. 2118.
Sheet III

Place	Date	Hour	Summary of Events and Information	Remarks and references to Appendices
H27b 65.70	July 24th contd		Q.A.D.M.S, D.A.D.O.S and S.S.O renown behind at RENINGHELST. O/C R.A. signal Office notified and 18th Div taking them traffic for Corps and beyond	
	25th		All men out on buried lines, repairing and trenching	
	26th		do	
	27		do 81452 Cpl J.T. WINSTANLEY awarded military medal for gallantry in action. maintenance of buried route. Fullerphone working to Bayouts in particularly do Fullerphone intentionally during to Eng lines. do Army forward lines	
	28		do	
	29th		do	
	30th		Attack at 3.5.0 am. Good speaking to 21st and 30th Bdes; intermittent speech to Bdes. Bde. rail forward lines but owing to heavy shelling keys were little use. 2nd Lt. R.P. HEPBURN M.C. wounded.	
	31st		Linemen have had very hard and continuous work nearly up the furthest system and also in supervising the working parties. Three casualties occurred. Sergt WILSON, L/Cpl M HARTON and Spr EXTON. Very good work done by all.	

WAR DIARY

OF THE

30th DIVISIONAL SIGNAL COMPANY

FOR

AUGUST 1917

September 1st 1917.

Capt. R.E.
O.C. 30th Divisional Signal Coy. R.E.

WAR DIARY
INTELLIGENCE SUMMARY.

Army Form C. 2118.

Sheet No. 1

Place	Date 1917	Hour	Summary of Events and Information	Remarks and references to Appendices
H.27.b.65.70 sheet 28 1/40,000	Aug 1st		Fighting still proceeds. Considerable trouble but communication continues. Brigades working mostly round and runners from captured positions. Only this Brigade in 90th Division being relieved by P.9.17. Very heavy work made communication very difficult. Lines become very full earth and works very hard to keep up. 2Lt R.P. HEPBURN died of wounds in No.10 C.C.S. His death is a great loss to the company.	
	3rd			
	3rd			
RENINGHELST	4th	6am	Advanced Div'l HQ at H.27.b.65.70 closed and reopened. Div'l HQ all at RENING HELST. 18" Division took over whole line morning. 30th Div. R.F.A. Bties. During the fighting July 31st to Aug 3rd communication with Bdes was kept going continuously by phone, telephone & runner, wireless. In front of Brigade communication presents very great difficulty as the shelling was very heavy all along. The 90th Bde did but established Forward Station on any lines as hooked by wire to one battalion and by runner. Both the 21st and 89th Brigades did forward both their own were in pre-arrangement

WAR DIARY
or
INTELLIGENCE SUMMARY.
(Erase heading not required.)

Army Form C. 2118.

Sheet II

Place	Date 1917	Hour	Summary of Events and Information	Remarks and references to Appendices
GODEWAERSVELDE	Aug 5th		Office at RENINGHELST closed 10 am and opened at GODEWAERSVELDE at same hour. Division comes under 9th Corps.	
	6th		R/mr GOWAN rejoined from Base Depot. Division resting	
	7th			
MERRIS	8th		Office at GODEWAERSVELDE closed 10 am and opened at MERRIS at same hour. Division resting	
	9th		do J. Wieler acting to course at 1st Corps. 30.R. to cable jointing course do 10.R. – instrument course do	
	10th		2/Lt G.G. COCHRAN R.E. joined for duty. 2/Lt GRICE attached from 17th Krrp J. Wieler duty on leave.	
	11th		Overhauling stores etc. Captain DARUISON on leave in England	
			Office at MERRIS closed 6 pm and entered at ST JAN CAPPEL at same hour. Comms to all Bdes, routes and Phone.	
ST JAN CAPPEL	12th		Division resting and overhauling. MDRs being taught overcoming breakers etc.	
	13th		do	
	14th			
	15th		do	
	16th			
	17th			

Army Form C. 2118.

WAR DIARY
or
INTELLIGENCE SUMMARY.
(Erase heading not required.)

Sheet 117

Instructions regarding War Diaries and Intelligence Summaries are contained in F. S. Regs., Part II. and the Staff Manual respectively. Title pages will be prepared in manuscript.

Place	Date 1917	Hour	Summary of Events and Information	Remarks and references to Appendices
51st JAN CAPPEL	Aug 18th		Division Resting. Training carried on.	
	19th		do do do	
	20th		do do do	
	21		Lt McGOWAN left unit and joined 2 Army Signal School	
	22		Captain Allison from leave	
			2/Lt GRICE rejoined his unit 17th Kings from doing wireless with Coy.	
	23	10 am	Office closed and opened at ULSTER CAMP DRANOUTRE	
ULSTER CAMP DRANOUTRE			21 Bde in line at RICHMOND DUGOUTS.	
			90 - support at KEMMEL	
			89 - reserve at DRANOUTRE.	
			11 Lt. Scattergood leave to UK.	
			Captain ANNEN from leave to UK	
	24th		Lt. G.R.T. WATKINS-PITCHFORD joined unit from 10th Corps wireless section	
	25th		Picking up cable; maintenance work. Establishing wireless	
	26		Church parade. Half holiday. do	
	27		Picking up cable	

A 5834 Wt. W4973 M687 750,000 8/16 D. D. & L. Ltd. Forms/C.2118/13.

Army Form C. 2118.

WAR DIARY
or
INTELLIGENCE SUMMARY.

Sheet IV

(Erase heading not required.)

Place	Date	Hour	Summary of Events and Information	Remarks and references to Appendices
DRANOUTRE	Aug 28		Capt. T.S. COLE M.C. RE(SR) joined Coy from I Corps Sig Sy. Picking up cable	
	29		Picking up cable. Arranging tours for another Both on tour	
	30		90 p Both on tour at NORTH MIDLAND FARM	
	31		Maj B. HOWARTH Offr Cg for 3rd Army Sig School.	

SECRET.

Vol 23

30TH DIVISIONAL SIGNAL COMPANY - ROYAL ENGINEERS.

------ W A R   D I A R Y ------

for the month of

SEPTEMBER, 1917.

VOLUME XXIII.

[signature]
Major, R.E.,
O.C.30th Div.Sig.Coy.R.E.

3-10-17.

Army Form C. 2118.

Sheet 1

WAR DIARY
or
INTELLIGENCE SUMMARY.
(Erase heading not required.)

Instructions regarding War Diaries and Intelligence Summaries are contained in F. S. Regs. Part II. and the Staff Manual respectively. Title pages will be prepared in manuscript.

Place	Date	Hour	Summary of Events and Information	Remarks and references to Appendices
DRANOUTRE	Sept 1		Picking up cattle. Arranging to take over Outpost from 37th Div.	
	2		89th Bde from KEMMEL to ONRAET FARM. 90th Bde from NORTH MIDLAND FARM	
	3		to KEMMEL.	
	4		Arranging mounted orders for KEMMEL Hill to HQrs of Bns & Battns in the line still kept	
	5		remaining for time available to 89th Bde for experience in the outpost.	
			90th outpost detailed, & moved into Gully road leading two brigades for parties	
	6		Maintenance of moved orders	
	7		1st 2nd MG & Signals	
	8		Maintenance of Bn & Units	
			do	
	9		do	
	10		do	
			to land relieving parties of 37th Div. 90th Bde also took over left of 89 Bde on the	
			left.	
	11		Headquarters opened next morning of 11/9/17	
			89th Bde deemed this over HD & now HD at ONRAET FARM arriving 5th.	
	12		8th Bde deemed this over were HQ 6 now HQ N.17.d.5.0 & late Bde Sig. Of	
			2/M.G. opened as Report Centre. Two Bdes of artillery on W.17.d.3.0. Of	

Army Form C. 2118.

WAR DIARY
or
INTELLIGENCE SUMMARY.
(Erase heading not required.)

Instructions regarding War Diaries and Intelligence Summaries are contained in F. S. Regs., Part II. and the Staff Manual respectively. Title pages will be prepared in manuscript.

Place	Date	Hour	Summary of Events and Information	Remarks and references to Appendices
DRANOUTRE	13		89th Bde HQ moved to new HQ 8.30 pm 9th line of hills at J.11.1 at V.D. Tel line yet through to B.F. lire.	
	14		Maintenance on Bundell Route. Brigade commenced J.27.d.5.0 to J.24.d.9 & Bde in intercommunication.	
	15		Buried field cable into farm J.26.d.2½.4½ HQ & MTC 2 ? O for no on work available. 9 hrs on work.	
	16		-Do- Recovery cable between DAYLIGHT CORNER & V.C. Road	
	17		-Do- Recovery cables	
	18		Laying cable line from FLEA FARM to ONRAET FARM (Adv 89th Bde) for use of Div Reserve	
	19		Laying line from Rumour of War cage OOSTAVERNE WOOD to WH I.30.an line through Kemmel to KEMMEL and large in trays. Two pigeons also sent to the station for use of intelligence officer who arranged to forward them when carrying pigeons. from Gp of FARM to Div CP at O.20.c.1.6 (Sheet 28 SW 2) also to FLEA FARM 2 and about 2.89th Bde in extension to Div CP on Bde CP line. 24 pigeons provided for use of IX Corps Intelligence.	
	20		Running through cable to Jimmy Stephen at Rumour of War cage. Battle commenced. Nothing of interest except as regards pigeons. See Journal	

Army Form C. 2118.

WAR DIARY
or
INTELLIGENCE SUMMARY.
(Erase heading not required.)

Place	Date	Hour	Summary of Events and Information	Remarks and references to Appendices
DRANOUTRE	21		Receipt of Orders for Proposed off Move Coys. & moving through reserve trenches.	
	22		Strengthening trenches made D.W. to R.V. 90th Bde relieved 89th Bde with Rest 21st Bde took over Bn Sector & 89th Bde moved into reserve area. All changes subsequently completed.	
	23		Overhauling & checking stores & clearing of dugouts, Bn hand over from IX to VIII Corps	
	24		Ditto	
	25		Strengthening of forward cable route to DRANOUTRE & running through cable	
	26		Nothing to report	
	27		30th Bde Sunday relieved 21st Bde taking over another by Cable to the H.Qrs. Necessary changes in Bn G/2 communication carried out. Recovering cable in neighbourhood of Curd Farm	
	28		Continued clearing Gay Farm area.	
	29		Ditto	
	30		Running through cable.	

SECRET.

No 24

30TH DIVISIONAL SIGNAL COMPANY - ROYAL ENGINEERS.
xxxxxxxxxxxxxxxxxxxxxxxxxxxxxxxxxxxxxxxxxxxx

W A R   D I A R Y

for the month of

OCTOBER 1917.

VOLUME XXIV.

4-11-17.

[signature]
Capt. R.E.,
A/O.C.30th Div.Sig.Coy.R.E.

Army Form C. 2118.

WAR DIARY
or
INTELLIGENCE SUMMARY.
(Erase heading not required.)

SHEET 1.

Instructions regarding War Diaries and Intelligence Summaries are contained in F.S. Regs., Part II. and the Staff Manual respectively. Title pages will be prepared in manuscript.

Place	Date	Hour	Summary of Events and Information	Remarks and references to Appendices
DRANOUTRE	October 1		Continued clearing 9 m/m 9 am line of cable – running thro' cable – repaired down of Lear dug-outs	
	2		Renewed cable in DRANOUTRE Area – running thro' cable	
	3		Continued thro' running thro' cable	
	4		Re-labelling all divisional overhead wire – running thro' cable	
	5		Running thro' cable	
	6		Commenced uncovering all un-labelled lines in divisional area in accordance with an order issued to all concerned.	
	7		Continued uncovering all cables (unlabelled) – Div. Bomb Store orders Reserve B 5th Dr.	
	8		do.	
	9		do.	
	10		do. 90th Inf Bde. relieving 31st & 3rd Bdes in Aspen Sector of line	
	11		do.	
	12		do. Above relief completed	

Army Form C. 2118.

SHEET 2

WAR DIARY
or
INTELLIGENCE SUMMARY.
(Erase heading not required.)

Instructions regarding War Diaries and Intelligence Summaries are contained in F. S. Regs., Part II. and the Staff Manual respectively. Title pages will be prepared in manuscript.

Place	Date	Hour	Summary of Events and Information	Remarks and references to Appendices
TRANDUINE	October 13		Continued weaving untested cable – reconnoitred route from Forest Farm to Grand Bois for burying cable to new Brigade H/qtrs – 21 hrs ? near line required – announced 9pm will be used – route taped out – work to be done in day time – 8 am to 1.0 pm	
	14		Commenced above route – a working party of 100 men supplied by 2nd Bn Bedfordshire Regt for this work – 220 yds cable buried 6" – 30 mm of this party continually employed in pumping out shell holes.	
	15		Major T. S. Coles M.O. R.E (S.R.) for leave to UK for 10 days – Capt D'Allison performing his duties – continued burying to Grand Bois – 40 yds cable buried 6" – same party employed on pumping	
	16		Continued burying – 110 yds cable buried 6" – 30 mm on pumping & 50 mm employed on "fanteen" ? burying 1' deep – working party supplied by 19 Bn KLR	
	17		Continued burying – 110 yds buried 6" – same parties employed as yesterday	
	18		do	do	

Army Form C. 2118.

WAR DIARY
or
INTELLIGENCE SUMMARY.
(Erase heading not required.)

SHEET 3

Place	Date 1917	Hour	Summary of Events and Information	Remarks and references to Appendices
DRANOUTRE	Oct 19		Continued firing from DRANOUTRE FARM & GRAND BOIS - 2.30 p.m. burst 6'2" wounded pvte. from By 19 Bn. K.L.R.	
	20		21st Bn By. regtl. shoot 9.0 a.m. Bell on Tiger Farm & ford. Slow daily completed - hung all cable buried & fallen in communication trenches. Bury ports 6 furnaces.	
	21		Same Bn above Bury BGRR - same intn. shoot, the emplacements & EK positions below Steam shed.	
	22		Removed brass from 9.15 & 9.F. Tear Boxes - alterations complete - drawing completed.	
	23		Nothing to report.	
	24		29 rounds aimed from Ad NAPA on NY 81.5.4 in new hollow in Grand Bois (N17.24.51).	
	25		Aimed at new positions at 4.p.m. all times OK. Formal strafe working. 10/1st SCATTERERS returned from monthly wireless course from Reserve Bgts. & - 6 should be Retransmitted north for new Tunnel (Textual) from DENNY HOUSE. The DENNY WOOD Tunnel have to be constructed by VIII Corps - reconnaissance & taking over new tunnel from DENNY WOOD.	
	26		Tour line to Bn HQrs. in DENNY WOOD was to be completed. 1st Division - Lt GUMPRED on down here trust from 2nd Gds. ASR & CHINESEWALL & 2/6 WILTSHIRE REGIMENT - commenced work.	
	27		Aug to DENNY WOOD - working party formed by 1st Bn. Transportation working to be shift of 15 min work - 9.5.30 to 9.30 - 9.30 a.m. completion 6 funnel up to about 2.0am. Field cable line breakdown from 3 Cons. in R.S. Lane (Tunnel Bn.) at BELGIAN Camp base to BELGIAN light by Regents dugouts.	

A.5834. Wt.W.4973 M687. 750,000 8/16 D.D.&L.Ltd. Forms/C.2118/13.

WAR DIARY
or
INTELLIGENCE SUMMARY

Army Form C. 2118.

SHEET

Place	Date 1917	Hour	Summary of Events and Information	Remarks and references to Appendices
DRAVOUTRE	28		continued burying from Dim Trench Road to Pm Hughes in DENYS WOOD - digging trench completed by 100 men of 17 En Hampshire Regt - burn covered by 3-9-7 pm am I three permanent cable the causalities	
	29	noon	got 25/links BGHa relieving 21st BGHa on right sector by home above relief completed at 12.15 noon employed on bombing up new burn.	
	30	day	all punts made a few panels fixed on above burn.	
		night	14 men employed on bombing up new burn	
	31		above burn completed & tested OK	

WAR DIARY

30th DIVISIONAL SIGNAL COMPANY R.E.

for the month of

NOVEMBER 1917.

Major R.E.
O.C. 30th Divisional Signal Coy. R.E.

Army Form C. 2118.

WAR DIARY
or
INTELLIGENCE SUMMARY.
(Erase heading not required.)

SHEET No. 1.

Place	Date 1917	Hour	Summary of Events and Information	Remarks and references to Appendices
DRANOUTRE	Nov 1st		Work in camp - draining &c - DW-DQ Lines strengthened ar wire renewing	
	2nd		Work in camp - draining &c.	
	3rd		do	
	4th	night	One officer & 1 NCO took charge of new lines from TORREKEN FARM to PRINCE RUPERTS DUGOUTS for VIII Corps	
	5th		Drainage of Camp &c -	
	6th		Continued improvement of Camp - draining & strengthening "B3" line wire in forward area.	
	7th		do.	
	8th		do	do - 2nd & 90th Bdes relieving 91st Bde in support sector of line	
	9th		do	do - above relief completed
	10th		do	do
	11th		do	do 90th Inf Bde moved to STRAZEELE area relieved by 14th Aus Inf Bde.

Army Form C. 2118.

WAR DIARY
or
INTELLIGENCE SUMMARY.

SHEET No 2

(Erase heading not required.)

Instructions regarding War Diaries and Intelligence Summaries are contained in F. S. Regs., Part II. and the Staff Manual respectively. Title pages will be prepared in manuscript.

Place	Date 1917	Hour	Summary of Events and Information	Remarks and references to Appendices
DRANOUTRE	Nov 12		Improvements in dugouts in forward areas completed. Portion of our front line North of the HOLLEBEKE – LOCRE road handed over to 37th Division, the line northern boundary now being from HOLLEBEKE along road through O.10.b.57.52 to its junction with the DAMM STRASSE at O.4.c.45.41	
	13.		Nothing over with to St Anne Division. An new party of 5 men sent to STEENVOORDE to prepare Signal Office etc.	
	14		21st Infantry Bgde from right centre to Hazzue Bgde area : 90th Infantry Bgde from STRAZEELE to STEENVOORDE	
STEENVOORDE	15		Coy moved from DRANOUTRE to STEENVOORDE. Office closed at DRANOUTRE 10am. Opened STEENVOORDE same time. 21st Btn officer opened STEENVOORDE 11am. No further returned from leave. Straightening up new office.	
	16		H.Q. Div Arty moved to METEREN. Communication established through METEREN	
	17		exchange	
	18		2/Lt Coenegan proceeded on leave. Training Signal Personnel in Linesman duties & infantry personnel in Power Buzzer Advance party proceeded to WESTOUTRE for taking over	
	19-23			
	24			
	25			
	26			

WAR DIARY
or
INTELLIGENCE SUMMARY.

SHEET No 3

Place	Date	Hour	Summary of Events and Information	Remarks references Appendi
WESTOUTRE	27		Office closed STEENVOORDE 10am, same hour opened WESTOUTRE, relieving 39th Div.	
	28		Work on front line commenced. Bivvies in bad condition.	
	29		Reviwit front exchange & purged out North East flanco or JF + YEDAVRY Batt.	
	30		Work continued on front trench mats, principally endeavring. Stuck. Work on JF - YP ≡ & D - HC mats both Zyll obs by enzymeleans.	

YM 26

30TH DIVISIONAL SIGNAL COMPANY - ROYAL ENGINEERS.

W A R   D I A R Y

for

DECEMBER 1917.

VOLUME XXVI.

J. Cole.
Major, R.E.,
O.C.30th Div.Sig.Coy.R.E.

4-1-18.

Army Form C. 2118.

WAR DIARY
or
INTELLIGENCE SUMMARY.
(Erase heading not required.)

Instructions regarding War Diaries and Intelligence Summaries are contained in F. S. Regs., Part II. and the Staff Manual respectively. Title pages will be prepared in manuscript.

Place	Date	Hour	Summary of Events and Information	Remarks and references to Appendices
WESTOUTRE	DEC 1		Work continued on trenches to obtain good glacis at Bn HQ at Derby Castle = 5 Period of alternative works being arranged	
	2		Work on trenches continued	
	3		Ditto	
	4		89th Bde HQ relieved 90th Bde HQ in the line. Bde groups relieved and came home. Method of holding line being one 1 Bde HQ in the line with 2 groups & Bn HQ the remaining 2 Bdes forming the new fight sector and 1 Bn HQ the third with HQ they in rear. This system enables much extra fight men & ammunition and 1 Bdr & group and very shortly under these an Bde HQ mountainly mud tramways between Bdes & Relieved Division 90 Cochran returned from leave	
	5		Working parties sorts & preparing billets at Bedford House for Relieved Detachment.	
	6		Ditto	
	7		Ditto	
	8		Adv Detachment under 2/Lt Cochrane proceeded to Bedford House & Commenced preparing an Advanced Divisional Cottage There to replace	

Army Form C. 2118.

WAR DIARY
or
INTELLIGENCE SUMMARY.
(Erase heading not required.)

Instructions regarding War Diaries and Intelligence Summaries are contained in F. S. Regs., Part II. and the Staff Manual respectively. Title pages will be prepared in manuscript.

Place	Date	Hour	Summary of Events and Information	Remarks and references to Appendices
WESTOUTRE	8		The exchange in SCOTTISH WOOD over from 89th Div. Work continued on maintenance of trench	
	9		Ditto	
	10		Ditto	
	11		Ditto	
	12		Night 12th/13th forward exchange moved from SCOTTISH WOOD to BEDFORD HOUSE 2.20. Line found connected from left of the Brigade.	
	13		21st Bde + No 2 front relieved 89th Bde + No 1 front in the line. Officers started opened LOVEOOTEN + STIRLING CASTLE regulating 10am. 90th Bde HQ taken over. Reconn. party. Necessary changes in lines at Lo COYTE made.	
	14		Work continued on buried routes + enforcing Arlo Exchange	
	15		Ditto	
	16		" Lt. G.R.J. WATKINS, PITCHFORD & hospitalised	
	17		Maintenance of front routes	
	18		Ditto	
	19		90th Inf. Bde + No 1 front relieved 21st Bde + No 2 front.	
	20		Decided that front system not to be continued & that in future time would be	

WAR DIARY
or
INTELLIGENCE SUMMARY.
(Erase heading not required.)

Army Form C. 2118.

Place	Date	Hour	Summary of Events and Information	Remarks and references to Appendices
WESTOUTRE	21		Held by two Bdes with one in reserve. Bde on rt told a m. Eastern front. Relieve other Bde. The other three Bdes to refine each other on the Western Lobby a two Bde front. BEDFORD HOUSE front open as Rt Bde HQ. Arranging communication for Rt Bde. Decided for simplicity to establish Brigade exchange at W.S. to avoid having large numbers of long lines out. First known means of transport available. Lt. S(east) F.H. DAWSON & Lt G.R.J. WATKINS-PITCHFORD marked in the photo.	
	22		21st Bde opened BEDFORD HOUSE 10 a.m. & took over Ad. Div Exchange. 89th Bde opened STIRLING CASTLE 10 a.m. 90th Bde opened La CLYTTE CAMP 10 a.m. All changes smoothly carried out. Nothing to report. Lt PITCHFORD reported sick.	
	23			
	24		All ordolacka men called in for Xmas Xmas preparations	
	25		Only necessary office work carried on. Dinners & entertainments. 90th Bde relieved 89th Bde	
	26		Work resumed on forced ends & clearing tunnels at TOR TOP & MOUNT SORREL	
	27		of storm center	
	28		Ditto	
	29		Ditto	
	30		Ditto	
	31		89th Inf Bde relieved 90th Inf Bde at STIRLING CASTLE.	

SECRET.

30TH DIVISIONAL SIGNAL COMPANY - ROYAL ENGINEERS.

W A R   D I A R Y

for

JANUARY 1918.

VOLUME XXVII.

Major, R.E.,
O.C. 30th Div. Sig. Coy. R.E.

2-2-1918.

WAR DIARY or INTELLIGENCE SUMMARY

Army Form C. 2118.

Place	Date	Hour	Summary of Events and Information	Remarks and references to Appendices
WESTOUTRE	1/1/1918		Work on brick walls, filling in shell holes on St-Y road, & other minor work in Dormy House area. Visited 20th Div Sigs to make preliminary arrangements for relay of work continued on maintenance of tracks	
	2		Ditto	
	3		Advance party of 39th Div. arrived. Woodcote, Bodyloyer & Paris Bridges maintenance	
	4		4 personnel at STIRLING CASTLE relieved	
	5		Location of establishment. A/W party of BEDFORD HOUSE relieved by 20 Div personnel. Three changed over in stretcher party at Bedford House relieved. Div R.E. moved to MORBECQUE & 90th Bde from LA CLYTTE to WATOU HYER. 60th Bde arrived LA CLYTTE & 61st Bde ZEVECOTEN. 20th Div Arty arrived WESTOUTRE in relief of our own.	
	6		Relief continued. Transport moved forward. Offr BLERINGHEM 99th of DESNAEVISELDE. Offrs BLARINGHEM own town. Ca moved St Langolun town.	
	7		Offrs closed WESTOUTRE 10 am. Head BLARINGHEM own town. B Coy proceeded own offices by train & lorry. 287 Ty Coy & H.Q proceeded own officers & men by train & lorry. 287 Coy mechanical transport, their precaution convoy.	
	8		Difficulty with mechanical transport. Offrs closed BORBIE own town. Offrs closed BLARINGHEM midnight. Offrs closed STEENBECQUE. Stm knight Delayed at STEENBECQUE till day. Transport party & lorry on way on 4th	
	9		Officers to CORBIE arrived 4 am. Delayed at STEENBECQUE till day. accident. Entraining resumed 5 a.m. arrived 8 pm	

WAR DIARY
or
INTELLIGENCE SUMMARY.

(Erase heading not required.)

Army Form C. 2118.

Place	Date	Hour	Summary of Events and Information	Remarks and references to Appendices
	10		Entraining commenced STEENBECQUE 8am. Staff at CORBIE. Adv. party part of Communication with Corps (XIII) + 90th Bde. already in CORBIE. Remainder of 89 arrived 8pm	
	11		Settling down in CORBIE + arranging for communication to 21st Bde. MORLUIL + 89th Bde	
	12		FORT MANOIR	
			Bdes arrived + communication established	
	13		Adv. party Sigs. for NESLE at 10am Transport Sigs. 11:15am. Settling the night at RORIERES	
	14		Office closed CORBIE opened NESLE from Sig. entrained CORBIE 9.30am arrived NESLE 2pm. Telephone arranged and Bden.	
	15		} Nothing to report	
	16		}	
	17		}	
	18		Adv party proceeded to ERCHEU to arrange new office + communication	
	19		Office closed NESLE 10am Signal ERCHEU communication to 90th Bde at LIEBERMONT by mounted + telephone. Telephone only to 89th at BEAULIEU + 21st at FRENICHES through Signal exchange	
	20		Improving communications + signal office	
	21		do	

WAR DIARY or INTELLIGENCE SUMMARY

Army Form C. 2118.

Place	Date	Hour	Summary of Events and Information	Remarks and references to Appendices
	22		Nothing to report	
	23		Nothing to report. DesRowith party proceed to CHAUNY area to have speech & Boles to be fixed, one at SINCENY Sq N.S.E, one at Du HQ at QUIERZY, one N.of LE OISE and at LIEZ & one at QUIERZY Du HQ at ROUEZ. Du HQ about Sp't ROUEZ, and Bgd L OGNES int emmbarly employment and CHAUNY under Hg. III Corps Army and Hg	
	24		Adv. party proceeded to CHAUNY under 2/Lt Cochrane. III Corps Army and Hq would use CHAUNY Head exchange them at our S.Jn.	
			Sorting out CHAUNY office & lines in the area. Running Lines in from P/ DALION Church	
	25		— do —	
	26		Work continued	
	27		Office closed EREMEU 11am. Opened CHAUNY at 2 hour. 89th Bat CHAUNY Sq Res	
	28		SALENCY 21st Bde VILLEQUIER–AUMONT. 58 Du Bty attached to CHAUNY and at PIERREMOND. opened a HH using CHAUNY exchange	
	29		Ferrers a HH using CHAUNY exchange at LIEZ (LOUVRE) and at PIERREMOND Relief commenced. Arranged for new exchange as 2.10 am. Hill Search Rby & other on Carnechan Co Command of section placed apparently about twice exchanges especially to over this first initefficient efforts to provide very complained could be made as was RP of previous Coy owing the say Rety Phase Coy th. bon every meet line every search. Received by Capt Anglin Capt Adjut to Conv. & Q to RIVER. Office to open at 2 pm Tomorrow. Staff officer	
	30			
	31			

A5834 Wt.W4973/M687 750,000 8/16 D.D. & L. Ltd. Forms/C.2118/13.

Army Form C. 2118.

WAR DIARY
or
INTELLIGENCE SUMMARY. Shut 1

(Erase heading not required.)

Instructions regarding War Diaries and Intelligence Summaries are contained in F. S. Regs., Part II. and the Staff Manual respectively. Title pages will be prepared in manuscript.

Place	Date July	Hour	Summary of Events and Information	Remarks and references to Appendices
ROUEZ	1		Continued taking over trenches & canal from the French — French exchange being gradually	
	2		thrown & lines put through.	
	3		do	
	4		do	
	5		do	
	6		do	
	7		Relief started by 5th Div. personnel	
	8		Advanced parties left ROUEZ for ERCHED	
	9		Hqrs. left ROUEZ 11 noon — Arrived at ERCHED same p.m. — 27th Bgde at FOENICHES · 29th Bgde at BEAULIEU · 90 Bgde at LIDERMONT	

Army Form C. 2118.

WAR DIARY
or
INTELLIGENCE SUMMARY.

SHEET 2

(Erase heading not required.)

Instructions regarding War Diaries and Intelligence Summaries are contained in F.S. Regs., Part II. and the Staff Manual respectively. Title pages will be prepared in manuscript.

Place	Date	Hour	Summary of Events and Information	Remarks and references to Appendices
ERCHEU	10		Capt DALLISON returned from leave to U.K. - proceeded on works course	
	11		11/Lt LORD FM. proceed for duty from 5th Army Sig Coy	
	12		11/Lt SCATTERGOOD on leave to U.K.	
	13		nothing to report	
	14		Lt THOMPSON on leave to U.K. - 11/Lt COLMAN to 89th Bde to replace	
	15		Reconnoitred for building suitable for Bde Sig place - LANNOY FARM chosen	
	16		Major Cole M.C. to works hunting house at ABBEVILLE	
			Lt IBBOTSON to to works nr.	
	17		nothing to report	
	18		11/Lt COCHRAN a 110 mm # reported to A.D. Sigs 18 Corps for buying unit in own area - one battalion from Bde employed in keeping cable trenches from Bde HQ's formed	
	19		Preparing new Bde HQ's at HAM - 21 on Bde HQ's at VILLERS ST CHRISTOPHE - 89th Bde at FLUQUIÈRES	
			90th Bde at VAUX & HQ's O mil Divs units	
	20		90th Bde moved to HAM - communication from Divs -	

WAR DIARY or INTELLIGENCE SUMMARY

Army Form C. 2118.

Sheet 3

Place	Date Oct 1918	Hour	Summary of Events and Information	Remarks and references to Appendices
ERCHEU	20		Instructions for div Sig Class reported for duty - preparing LANNOY FARM for reoccupation by	
	21		2⁄Meulnis - continued work on all lines held by units	
	22		to comment on work alone	
			On complete offices about 2000 men to HAM for duties - relieved by 20th Division	
HAM	23		Office closed ERCHEU at 10.0 am & reopened in HAM at same hour - Staff moved to go to	
			DURY moved to VILLERS ST CHRISTOPHE - 21st Bgde moved to VILLERS ST CHRISTOPHE	
			84th Bgde to FLUQUIERES - 9th Bgde to VAUX - Bns held met one Bn/Bde in town on each	
			Bgde front - all lines through OK - corps building b/w route from DURY to AUBIGNY	
			LANNOY FARM reopened by 2030 for Bgde School - MOYENCOURT CHATEAU prepared to	
			where.	
	24		Commenced preparing arrangements airborne for Sig class - working party wiring DIRY roads for	
			Bn NylN	
	25		Continued work on above - baled out corps route from DURY to AUBIGNY - 2 hrs in contact - corps	
			linesmen out on faults - at 10.0 pm they reported three air cycle - both that given as being Li-	

WAR DIARY
or
INTELLIGENCE SUMMARY.

(Erase heading not required.)

Army Form C. 2118.

SHEET 4

Place	Date	Hour	Summary of Events and Information	Remarks and references to Appendices
HAM	25th		Pull in w/s same broke - a wiring party from corps was sent out - worked till 1 am - 2 am	
			but 3 pr still in contact - corps M/C also left with our mails party with orders	
	26		Corps mails not completed till 8-0 pm - Office Staff at HAM at 10-1 am & returned at DUEY	
			at same hour - had trying to into units with not being completed. W & W connection by trunk to get	
			Open at HAM with two trunks to DUEY - line worked units satisfactorily in spite of rain	
			caused no trouble -	
	AD Sep 10		Corps handed over lines from 9 Div & 6 with to 8 Sussex to complete -	
	27		Office at HAM closed down - all w/s lifted and on were made to POISOLY - visited being ground	
			stations & telephone staff moved there	
			Notice given by Staff of information of enemy as impending attack by the enemy on our front -	
			Working parties of 500 men throng cable trench from cable head to battalion HQ in strong points	
	MANCHESTER HILL			
	28		Continued work on above lines - working parties of 30 men on new line into Staff points at	

Army Form C. 2118.

WAR DIARY
or
INTELLIGENCE SUMMARY.
(Erase heading not required.) SHEETS

Instructions regarding War Diaries and Intelligence Summaries are contained in F.S. Regs., Part II. and the Staff Manual respectively. Title pages will be prepared in manuscript.

Place	Date	Hour	Summary of Events and Information	Remarks and references to Appendices
DURY	2 8 cont.		at L'EPINE DE DALLON – forward trench dug & cables down & tested OK but our future in – the latter been completed station OK – continued laying cable to OP's in latter "Strong Point" but not completed. Another circuit by different route from than to each Brigade in the line.	

SECRET.

30TH DIVISIONAL SIGNAL COMPANY - ROYAL ENGINEERS.

WAR DIARY

for the month of

MARCH 1918.

VOLUME XXIX.

5-4-18.

Major, R.E.,
O.C. 30th Div. Sig. Coy., R.E.

Army Form C. 2118.

WAR DIARY
or
INTELLIGENCE SUMMARY.
(Erase heading not required.)

Instructions regarding War Diaries and Intelligence Summaries are contained in F. S. Regs., Part II. and the Staff Manual respectively. Title pages will be prepared in manuscript.

Place	Date	Hour	Summary of Events and Information	Remarks and references to Appendices
DURY	1		Completed burying cable from cable head to MANCHESTER HILL (strong point) & continued work in Strong Point at L'EPINE de DALLON	
			As no troops yet formed in tropa area, returned in from Bn Hqrs at PERONNE? which also work sent to each of the battalions in the line - one M/L D.C. was also sent to each Bn.	
	2		for dumps back to Bn Hqtrs. - Prepared underground exposed dugouts at Bn Hqtrs. 30 shellings from each Bgde (90 mm) assembled at Underground entrances to be used instead of usual sprinkler. Completed trench at L'epine de Dallon - ditto OK	
	3		Carried on and traced work in DURY	
			LT WRIGHT on leave to PARIS - LT THOMPSON & 2/LT SCATTERGOOD returned from leave	
	4		Completed test boxes in burying PS: ML & connecting cable ends (m.L.) to D.P.s on Manchester Hill.	
	5		Buried two pairs from ML test box to Bgde OP on Manchester Hill - joined up AL cost point? 2 strengthened leading in cables - 150 men employed	
	6		Working party 150 men laying up burg PS: M.L - constructing two boxes & strengthening leading in at PS test point - buried cross pair on P note to PITMAN to take up Bn Tens & Coys. Receiving divinal cables.	

A 5834 Wt. W 4973/M687 750,000 8/16 D. D. & L. Ltd. Forms/C.2118/13.

Army Form C. 2118.

WAR DIARY
or
INTELLIGENCE SUMMARY.
(Erase heading not required.)

SHEET 2

Place	Date 1918	Hour	Summary of Events and Information	Remarks and references to Appendices
DURY	7		Continued work on P.S. - M.L. line - patching up damaged cables - 21" Bpk returned g.o Bpk in left sector. 11/1st Sussex Regt. left coy for duty at 5th Army.	
	8		Continued work at PN test box - at work AL test box - Jouncil forked route to CRE to replace damaged cable	
	9		Completed shifts over AL test box & stamping lines with sandbags. LT WRIGHT attached from Paris. Continued work at PN test box. Commenced convoy route from H.A.M. to BOUZE at BOULANCOURT - no other site available from the Army.	
	10		N Corps - completed test boxes on P.S.-M.L. line, & L.T.s available where buried by lorry. Continued work at P.N. dugout.	
	11		Continued route to GOLANCOURT - afflicting P.S.-M.L. line at test position forward line - ending 14 pts line & out of Italy in Brown Queen - Quarry 5 pairs through from P.S.-M.L. 120 men employed in two shifts - 9.30pm & 11.45pm - Commenced patch cable route from left Bpk dugout to VX test box to replace existing route to E.T. Last line from R.O.W. case at F1661.9 to N° Bpk St.	
	12		Completed work to Hamcourt - laid in cables at B.Q. test dug out, tested route K - constituent patch cable route to VX. Major Cole returned from leave.	

WAR DIARY
or
INTELLIGENCE SUMMARY.

Army Form C. 2118.

(Erase heading not required.)

Place	Date	Hour	Summary of Events and Information	Remarks and references to Appendices
DURY	13		Nothing to report	
	14		Ditto	
	15		Obtained cable reconnoitred routes for laying all lines into Div HQ	
	16		Commenced boring under roads & courtyard for laying into Div HQ.	
	17		Work continued	
	18		Working party digging trenches & laying out cable for above lines	
	19		Work continued. Ground cable laid as communication for Battle Zone defence tested	
	20		Warning received of impending attack. Lines laid onto Bde Battle HQ which though incomplete could be occupied if necessary.	
	21		Enemy attack opened at about 4.30 am. Warning had been given that attack might occur, and as it was not considered advisable to depend on excepting open line communication to Bdes, two cable detachments had been warned to be ready to run lines from AUBIGNY toward Bdes in the event. This turned most invaluable, as quite early Div HQ were shelled out all its permanent routes destroyed. The cable lines were kept though all day, and cable also laid into the route to Coopers & into the Flank Divisions. The line to Bde H.Q. at VAUX was lively cut about in the evening and was relaid	

Army Form C. 2118.

WAR DIARY
or
INTELLIGENCE SUMMARY.
(Erase heading not required.)

Instructions regarding War Diaries and Intelligence Summaries are contained in F. S. Regs., Part II. and the Staff Manual respectively. Title pages will be prepared in manuscript.

Places	Date	Hour	Summary of Events and Information	Remarks and references to Appendices
DURY	1918 Mar. 21		Workers and Power Buzzer did most valuable work in the forward area, especially in the right sector, where the forward lines were cut early in the attack. All W/T personnel in NANCHESTER HILL and EPIN de DALLON are missing. Five men in SAVY Dugouts were captured by enemy; subsequently they were recaptured and escaped, rejoining Company at HAM.	
HAM	22		H.Q. moved back to HAM about 6 a.m., and Batn Lines put through to Bdes. Exchange on existing lines back. About midnight Div. HQ moved back to ERCHEU, Bells moving to HQ on the second truck near LANOY FARM, communication being established by cable from ERCHEU.	
ERCHEU	23		H.Q. removed as above, and communication maintained by cable. Transport sent back to ROIGLISE and new office established. Cable run out from ERCHEU to ROIGLISE.	
SOLENTE	24		H.Q. moved back as far as SOLENTE, advanced office being left open at ERCHEU. Cable lines from ERCHEU to SOLENTE via new Bdes. HQ at 0.14.a. when all Bde. HQ collected. ERCHEU heavily shelled, and two men (Sgt. Owen and Pte. Dawson, 11 L.S. Lancs Regt.) wounded repairing lines. When office closed down and transferred to SOLENTE, new office in communication with Bdes. and all lines out forward, ERCHEU office closed down and transferred to SOLENTE.	

A 5834. Wt. W4973 M687 750,000 8/16 D. D. & L. Ltd. Forms/C.2118/13.

WAR DIARY
or
INTELLIGENCE SUMMARY.
(Erase heading not required.)

Army Form C. 2118.

Place	Date	Hour	Summary of Events and Information	Remarks and references to Appendices
ROIGLISE	13/8 Mar 25		H.Q. moved back to ROIGLISE about noon. Bttns also on move. Being relieved by 62nd French Division.	
HANGEST	26	About 10.30 am	H.Q. moved to HANGEST, and Bttns also moved to new area to rest.	
			H.Q. arrived HANGEST about 4.30 am. At 8.30 am orders given to take up position in front of HANGEST. 90th Bttn H.Q. established near AMIENS road and 89th Bttn at FOLIES. Cable laid to 90th Bttn. H.Q. and extended to 89th. 21st Bttn in reserve at HANGEST. Bttn. 87th Bttn moved back close to 90th Bttn., still keeping in communication on the cable line.	
BRACHES	27		New H.Q. established at BRACHES. Cable laid from HANGEST to BRACHES and run picked up there to Corps. G.O.C. remained forward near HANGEST until telephone laid into line, to enable him to keep in touch with Bttns and new, till evening. At night lived light with Bttns from BRACHES by this cable. Relief by 133rd French Division arranged. Cable remained though, though broken at times. Four men kept near HANGEST to insure repair. Relay out properly completed and Battalion in line. Later in morning elements of 30th Division still in line, relieved 20th Division by Corps. Bttns withdrew, and Lannemin restored to new	
ESTREE-SUR-NOYE	28			

Army Form C. 2118.

Instructions regarding War Diaries and Intelligence Summaries are contained in F. S. Regs., Part II. and the Staff Manual respectively. Title pages will be prepared in manuscript.

WAR DIARY
or
INTELLIGENCE SUMMARY.
(Erase heading not required.)

Place	Date 1918	Hour	Summary of Events and Information	Remarks and references to Appendices
ESTREE-SUR-NOYE	Mar. 28		Enemy very close. All newspapers next day. In meantime, all transport and personnel except office staff had been moved to ROUVREL. HQ ordered to ESTREE-SUR-NOYE. Office closed at BRACHES and office staff moved direct to ESTREE by lorry, opening office on arrival. Line to AILLY exchange provided for communication to G.H.Q. and line from ROUVREL to AILLY pushed up and used for communication to all Groups in ROUVREL.	
	29		Office remained open at ESTREE. Rest of Company moved in from ROUVREL.	
ST VALERY-SUR-SOMME	30		Orders received at 8.30 am to move by 10.30 am to SALEUX, to entrain personnel to ST. VALERY-SUR-SOMME. Transport to go by road. Shortly after orders amended, and told to get off if no lorry as possible. Personnel to entrain at SALEUX at 3 am. Transport and all spare personnel moved about 10 am. Lorries and office staff remaining till about 1 pm, when office was closed, and remaining personnel proceeded in lorries to ST.VALERY, staying the night at ABBEVILLE.	
	31		Picked up line to SAIGNEVILLE exchange, subsequently extended to ABBEVILLE and put staff on exchange. Communication to Rear by D.R. only, as no lines available or required.	

SECRET.

30TH DIVISIONAL SIGNAL COMPANY - ROYAL ENGINEERS.

W A R   D I A R Y
for the month of
APRIL, 1918.

VOLUME XXX.

[signature]
Major, R.E.,
O.C. 30th Div. Sig. Coy. R.E.

5-5-18.

WAR DIARY
or
INTELLIGENCE SUMMARY.
(Erase heading not required.)

Army Form C. 2118.

Place	Date	Hour	Summary of Events and Information	Remarks and references to Appendices
ST.VALERY-SUR-SOMME	1		Nothing of interest to report	
	2		Transport arrived	
	3		Nothing to report	
	4		Commenced from ST.VALERY to WOINCOURT	
			Party on lorries sent on in advance to fix up communication	
			Party on lorries sent on in advance to fix up communication	
PROVEN	5		Office opened at PROVEN. Lt. IBBOTSON returned from leave	
	6		Train to be expected about 1 am. Advance party forwarded to CANAL BANK	
			to fix up new office ready to take over by actn. of 1st Dvn.	
	7		Arranging to take over from 1st Dvn.	
CANAL BANK	8		Office closed PROVEN 10am. reopened CANAL BANK 2pm Kinny 89" Bde in line	
			at VARNA FARM. 90th in support of FUSILIER HOUSE. 21st Bde in reserve near ELVERDINGHE Dvn HQ	
	9		Maintenance of buried cable. Wireless communication established between Dvn & Bgds + R.E Coy in line	
	10		89' Bde to front B.Hzat SOUVENIR and Bridges + Pone Byzar & R.E Coy in line	
	11		Maintenance of lines continued	
	12		Dvn office opened at ELVERDINGHE Chateau 3pm	
ELVERDINGHE	13		Commenced to move of what of Dvn HQ to ELVERDINGHE	
			Office closed CANAL BANK 2 pm. Coy transd to ELVERDINGHE in line. Strength of Coy	
			89th Bde buried cable to MORBEL FM. 90 & B.Ht Killing Lane VARNA forward system + B.H.C 192	

WAR DIARY or INTELLIGENCE SUMMARY

Army Form C. 2118.

Place	Date	Hour	Summary of Events and Information	Remarks and references to Appendices
ELVERDINGHE	14		Rear office opened at ST SIXTE	
	15		Arranging for distribution of forward parties on withdrawal of 1st & 2nd Bn R.B's	
	16		Destruction of forward dumps completed. Attendance party left at Canal Bank to maintain remaining services front of canal.	
	17		Arranging for relief of 5th L.R. Bde Gen. Div. 89th Bde already left Div other place in support taken by 21st Bde	
BUSSEBOOM	18		Div HQ moved to BUSSEBOOM. Landmark started in & actual starting up near H.Q. Temporarily took over of rear office of ST SIXTE. In afternoon MOONTA CAMP occupied & communication with Corps and 90th Bde established. Motor company except officers left at ST SIXTE ordered to MOONTA food tents transport & supplies personnel included that to ST SIXTE	
	19		90th & 21st Bdes confined in one envelope Bde under O.C. 21st Bde 21st Bde Off. 21st Andrew sector of the line coming under 21st Div	
	20		90th Bde HQ with 2 Bns BdHd HQ moved to LEDERZEELE. Communication to Pilkeith Army Corps & & from St SIXTE offices at G.	
	21		Div HQ moved to ERIE CAMP Bring forward stores from SIXTE efford within to relief	

WAR DIARY
or
INTELLIGENCE SUMMARY.
(Erase heading not required.)

Army F

Instructions regarding War Diaries and Intelligence Summaries are contained in F. S. Regs., Part II. and the Staff Manual respectively. Title pages will be prepared in manuscript.

Place	Date	Hour	Summary of Events and Information	Re. refe. App.
BUSSBOOM	22		Military Target	
	23		"	
	24		"	
	25		"Q" moved to LEDERZEELE area. Transport moved by road train places staying nights at PROVEN	
	26		"G" with advanced Div remained at WIERE. Remaining reached BROXEELE & opened new office	
	27		Advanced office closed & Div moved to BROXEELE	
BROXEELE	27		Arranging fresh HQ at Huby P20c32. All offices opened in the evening	
	28		G & CRE moved to Adv. HQ. Remainder at BROXEELE	
	29		Situation unchanged	
	30		The following Awards have been made during the month:—	
			Lieut. J. W. Wright R.S.F. Military Cross	
			A/Sgt. G. H. Kent R.E. ⎤	
			16380 Cpl. D. E. Ferguson R.E. ⎥ Never brought forward	
			142800 " G. H. Clarkson R.E. ⎬ For gallant & distinguished	
			312768 Spr. J. Praytor R.E. ⎥ conduct.	
			81424	
			311252 Pnr. C. Enlick R.E. Military Medal	

SECRET

30TH DIVISIONAL SIGNAL COMPANY - ROYAL ENGINEERS.

WAR DIARY

for the month of

MAY, 1918.

VOLUME XXXI.

[signature]
Major, R.E.,
O.C. 30th Div.Sig.Coy.R.E.

1-6-18.

WAR DIARY
or
INTELLIGENCE SUMMARY.

(Erase heading not required.)

Army Form.

Instructions regarding War Diaries and Intelligence Summaries are contained in F. S. Regs., Part II. and the Staff Manual respectively. Title pages will be prepared in manuscript.

Place	Date	Hour	Summary of Events and Information	Remarks referen. Appenn.
BROXEELE	MAY 1		Nothing to report.	
	2		Nothing to report.	
	3		Nothing to report.	
	4		Nothing to report.	
	5		1st Advanced Div. H.Q. moves from CASSEL to WATOU.	
	6		Nothing to report.	
	7		do	
	8		do	
	9		do	
	10		Advanced Div. H.Q. returned to BROXEELE.	
	11		CAPT. DALLISON proceeded to EU.	
	12		Nothing to report.	
	13		Advanced Party proceeded to EU	
	14		Nothing to report.	
	15		do	
EU	16		Coy moves to EU entraining at WOINCOURT at 4. a.m. on the 16th Signal Office at BROXEELE closes at 10 p.m. 15.5.18. Transport lines at ST. QUENTIN LAMOTTE 21st BDE at BAROMESNIL. 89th BDE at TULLY 90th BDE Bgt left joining XXII Corps on defence work.

WAR DIARY
INTELLIGENCE SUMMARY.
(Erase heading not required.)

Army Form C. 2118.

Place	Date	Hour	Summary of Events and Information	Remarks and references to Appendices
E.V. (cont)	17		Nothing of note to report. [35TH AMERICAN DIVISION affiliated to 30TH DIVISION (BRITISH) for training purposes. H.Q. of former also at F.V.]	
	18		do	
	19		90th Inf. Bde. took over from 21st Inf. Bde. at BAROMESNIL; 21st Bde. H.Q. to BEAUMONT CHATEAU	
	20		Company training commenced. Wireless Section under Lieut. Pitchford. No 1 Section under 2.Lt. G.C. Cochran. No 5 " " 2 Lt. F.M. Lord.	
			2 Lieut Cochran went up to line at ST. QUENTIN-LAMOTTE, where the training took place.	
	21		Nothing to report. Company training continues	
	22		Ditto	
	23		Ditto	
	24		Ditto	
	25		Ditto	
	26		CAPT. DALLISON left Company for duty with VII Corps Signals.	
	27		21st BDE SIGNAL SECTION left BEAUMONT CHATEAU to join 21st BDE H.Q. and proceeded to HUPPY to form 33RD AMERICAN DIVISION.	
	28		Company training still proceeding; nothing else to report.	
	29		Ditto	
	30		Ditto	
	31		Ditto	

SECRET.

30TH DIVISIONAL SIGNAL COMPANY → ROYAL ENGINEERS.

WAR DIARY

for the month of

JUNE 1918.

VOLUME XXXII.

1-7-18.

[signature] Major, R.E.
O.C. 30th Div. Sig. Coy., R.E.

WAR DIARY
or
INTELLIGENCE SUMMARY

JUNE 1918.

Place	Date	Hour	Summary of Events and Information	Remarks and references to Appendices
F.U.	1		Company training continued at ST. QUENTIN-LAMOTTE.	
	2		The following N.C.O's and men of this unit have been awarded the MILITARY MEDAL.	
			No. 83055 a/Cpl JONES, H.	
			No. 142800 M/Cpl. FERGUSON, D.C.	
			No. 83478 Spr. ATKINS, T.	
			No. 16380 a/Sgt KENT, G.H.	
			No. 81427 Spr. NAYLOR, F.	
			CAPT. C.T. CRANSWICK R.E. joined this unit for duty from the 57th DIV (ARTY) (SIGS)	
	3		Nothing to report.	
	4		Ditto.	
	5		CAPT. F.H. DALLISON R.E awarded the MILITARY CROSS.	
	6		Nothing to report.	
	7		35th AMERICAN DIVISION left this area.	
	8		Operating and maintenance.	
	9		Ditto.	

WAR DIARY
INTELLIGENCE SUMMARY

Army Form C. 2118.

Place	Date	Hour	Summary of Events and Information	Remarks and references to Appendices
EU (cont)	10		Operating and maintenance.	
	11		33rd AMERICAN DIVISION moved to this area from HUPPY area.	
	12		21st INF. BDE left HUPPY and proceeds to MONCHAUX.	
	13		Operating and maintenance	
	14		SIGNAL BATT. of 33rd AMERICAN DIVN. arrived at EU.	
	15		Operating and maintenance.	
	16		Ditto	
	17		Ditto. LT. C.A. WEBSTER (M.G.C.) joined this unit and was posted as Signal Officer to No. 5 SECTION.	
	18		Orders received for 30TH DIVISION to move to RUE area.	
	19		CAPT. C.T. CRANSWICK and one Officer relief proceeds to RUE. 2.LT. G.G. COCHRAN proceeds to NOLETTES with transport. LT. C.A. WEBSTER proceeds to NOLETTES with marching party.	
	20		Move of Division to RUE area completed. H.Q. RUE. 21st BDE BEHEN. D/B. & L. I.M. Wforms/C2118/1 89th BDE PONTHOILE. 90th BDE to TULLY.	

Army Form C. 2118.

WAR DIARY
or
INTELLIGENCE SUMMARY
(Erase heading not required.)

Instructions regarding War Diaries and Intelligence Summaries are contained in F. S. Regs., Part II. and the Staff Manual respectively. Title pages will be prepared in manuscript.

Place	Date	Hour	Summary of Events and Information	Remarks and references to Appendices
RUE	21	—	Operating and maintenance.	
	22.		Lt. R. WATKINS-PITCHFORD proceeded on leave.	
	23.		Operating and maintenance	
	24.		Ditto.	
	25.		Box car (CROSSLEY) delivered to Company	
	26.		CAPT. C.T. CRANSWICK proceeds to EPERLEQUES with advance party.	
	27.		Signal office closes at RUE at 11.0 A.M. reopens at EPERLEQUES at the same hour. The 30th DIV. moves to EPERLEQUES area by train; entraining at RUE and detraining at AUDRICQ. Brigades situated as follows: 21st BDE. GANSPETTE 89th BDE. EPERLEQUES 90th BDE. SERQUES. — LT.J.W. WRIGHT proceeded on leave.	
	28.		Operating and maintenance	
	29.		ditto.	
	30.		"A" Section proceeded to EPERLEQUES; to be 30th M.G. Btt.	

SECRET.

30TH DIVISIONAL SIGNAL COMPANY - ROYAL ENGINEERS.

WAR DIARY
for the month of
J U L Y, 1918.

VOLUME XXXIII.

1-8-17.

[signature]
Major, R.E.,
O.C.30th Div.Sig.Coy., R.E.

Vol 33

WAR DIARY
or
INTELLIGENCE SUMMARY.

(Erase heading not required.)

Army Form C.-2118.

Place	Date	Hour	Summary of Events and Information	Remarks and references to Appendices
EPERLECQUES	JULY 1		Nothing of interest to report.	
	2		Operating and maintenance	
	3		ditto.	
	4		First issue of 2 light Cable Carts received.	
	5		Operating and maintenance.	
	6		Ditto	
	7		Ditto	
	8		Nos. 1 & 5 Sections, Wireless and Transport moved by road to CASSEL staying the night b/s at NIEULET. CAPT. CRANSWICK with one Officer relief proceeded straight to CASSEL to open up new Office.	
CASSEL	9		Signal Office closes at EPERLECQUES at 11.0 a.m. reopening at CASSEL at the same hour.	
	10.		2/Lt. LORD proceeds to No. 3 Section during leave to Lt. K. ALLWRIGHT.	
	11.		No. 5 Section issues 30 Bns of M.G.C.	
	12.			

Army Form C. 2118.

WAR DIARY
or
INTELLIGENCE SUMMARY.
(Erase heading not required.)

Instructions regarding War Diaries and Intelligence Summaries are contained in F.S. Regs., Part II. and the Staff Manual respectively. Title pages will be prepared in manuscript.

Place	Date	Hour	Summary of Events and Information	Remarks and references to Appendices
CASSEL (cont)	13		Lt. WRIGHT rejoined from leave to U.K.	
	14.		1st Course for Bn. Signallers in P.B.& A assembled: to last 1 week.	
	15.		2/Lt. COCHRAN proceeded to Adv. Div. H.Q. at STEENVOORDE with No.1. Section.	
	16.		Operating and maintenance	
	17.		Ditto	
	18.		Practice manning Battle Stations. Alarm given 1.46 a.m. Ceased 3.30 a.m.	
	19.		Nothing of interest to report. [2/Lt. LORD rejoined H.Q. from No. 3 Section	
	20.		2/Lt. COCHRAN proceeded on 14 days' leave to U.K.	
			2/Lt. LORD to Adv. Div. H.Q. to take over No.1. Section.	
	21.		2nd P.B.& A. Course assembled.	
	22.		Test Battle Orders received 12.3 p.m...	
			Establishment of Coy. increased by 3 DR's and 4 Operators, to be attached to Corps.	
			3 DR's and 3 Operators transferred from X Corps Sig. Coy. to this unit on 26-7-18	

Army Form C. 2118.

WAR DIARY
or
INTELLIGENCE SUMMARY.
(Erase heading not required.)

Place	Date	Hour	Summary of Events and Information	Remarks and references to Appendices
CASSEL (cont)	23		21ST BDE. H.Q. moved from ST. MARIE CAPPEL to P.7. L.2.9 (Sheet 27)	
	24.		SILENT PERIOD 6 a.m. to 6 p.m.	
	25.		ADV. DIV. moved from STEENVOORDE to TERDEGHEM.	
	26.		No 1. Section returned from ADV. DIV. H.Q.	
	27.		90TH BDE. H.Q. closed at 10 a.m. Places at disposal of 36TH Div. and relieved 106TH BDE, which was attached to 30TH Div.	
	28.		Operating & maintenance	
	29.		Inspection of the Company by the G.O.C.	
	30.		Operating and maintenance. CAPT. SAVILLE to hospital sick.	
	31.		LIEUT. J.F. ROXBURGH (Gen. List: T.F.) joined this unit for duty as supernumary from 2nd Army, and proceeded to 30TH D.A.	

SECRET.

WR 34

30TH DIVISIONAL SIGNAL COMPANY - ROYAL ENGINEERS.

WAR DIARY

for the month of

AUGUST 1918.

VOLUME XXXIV.

1-9-18.

S. Kaye-Lacy
Major, R.E.
O.C. 30th Divl. Signal Coy. R.E.

WAR DIARY or INTELLIGENCE SUMMARY

Army Form C. 2118.

Place	Date	Hour	Summary of Events and Information	Remarks and references to Appendices
CASSEL	AUGUST			
	1		SILENT DAY from 7 a.m to 7 p.m.	
	2		Advanced P & A Course commenced & last one week.	
	3		Nothing of interest to report.	
	4		2 Lt. G.G. COCHRAN rejoined from 14 days leave to U.K. Capt. R.W. Newman joined unit from 14th Div. Sig. Coy. R.E. and was posted to 30th D.A. vice Capt. SAVILLE. Lt. ROXBURGH proceeded to 90th Bde Sigs.	
	5		Operating and maintenance.	
	6		ditto.	
	7		ditto.	
	8		30th BRIT. DIV. Commenced relief of 35th BRIT. DIV. in LOCRE Sector.	
	9		Relief continued amongst units.	
	10		SILENT DAY from 7 a.m to 7 p.m. Signal office at CASSEL closed 10 a.m. and reopened at TERDEGHEM at	

Army Form C. 2118.

WAR DIARY
or
INTELLIGENCE SUMMARY.
(Erase heading not required.)

Place	Date	Hour	Summary of Events and Information	Remarks and references to Appendices
TERDEGHEM	10		CAPT. CRANSWICK and 2.Lt. COCHRAN proceeded to Adv Div Hqrs at MERTHKMME.	
	11.		Remaining personnel and transport proceeded by road to TERDEGHEM under 2Lt. F.M. FORD. Relief completed.	
	12		Operating and maintenance.	
	13		ditto.	
	14		ditto.	
			Major T.S. COLE M.C. R.E. proceeded to 2nd ARMY SIGNAL SCHOOL for a 7 days C.in.C. W/T Course.	
	15-19		Operating and Maintenance.	
	20.		Operating and maintenance.	
	21.		Attack by 50th Div: for report see summary attached.	
	22.		Lt. C.F. THOMPSON (50th BDE SIGS) wounded and proceeded to F.A. this day. Major T.S. COLE M.C. R.E. rejoined unit from course at 2nd ARMY SIGNAL SCHOOL Lt. ROXBURGH to 89th BDE SIGS.	
	23		Operating and maintenance.	

WAR DIARY
or
INTELLIGENCE SUMMARY.
(Erase heading not required.)

Army Form C. 2118.

Place	Date	Hour	Summary of Events and Information	Remarks and references to Appendices
TERDEGHEM	24		Operating and maintenance. Nothing of interest to report.	
	25		Ditto	
	26		Ditto	
	27		Major F. KAYE-PARRY. to take over to from Major COLE. M.C. R.E.	
	28		Nothing of interest to report.	
	29			
	30		Major F. KAYE PARRY R.E. 15th Command of Company.	
	31		Major T.S. COLE. M.C. R.E. to ENGLAND for duty with THAMES & MEDWAY defences.	
			Major F. KAYE PARRY to Adv. Div. (Capt. CRANSWICK to establish office at ROMANOS (MONT NOIR). SIGNAL OFFICE at TERDEGHEM closes at 6.30 p.m. Transport moved by road to MOUTON under 2nd Lt. LORD. MAJOR KAYE-PARRY R.E. and 2nd Lt. COCHRAN proceeds to Adv. Div at ROMANOS.	

SECRET.

30TH DIVISIONAL SIGNAL COMPANY - ROYAL ENGINEERS.

WAR DIARY

for the month of

SEPTEMBER 1918.

VOLUMN XXXV.

1-10-18.

Major, R.E.
O.C. 30th Divisional Signal Coy. R.E.

WAR DIARY
INTELLIGENCE SUMMARY

Army Form C. 2118.

SEPTEMBER

Place	Date	Hour	Summary of Events and Information	Remarks and references to Appendices
MONT VIDAIGNE	1		Transport moved from MOUTON (GODEWAERSVELDE Area) to Div. Rear HQ at LA MONTAGNE at 6.30 am under C.S.M. 2/Lieut. F.M. LORD + 4 Lin. men proceeded to Adv. Div. HQ. Lines laid to 21 Bde at BEAVER HALL DUGOUTS + to 89 Bde at FOXGLOVE FARM.	
	2		Transport under C.S.M. moved to MONT NOIR QUARRY. Line laid to ULSTER CAMP (28/M.35 c 2.5) for 89 Bde.	
	3		Remainder of Personnel, except Office Staff to Rear HQ, moved to ADV. HQ. Div HQ. moved from ROMANOS to SOVIET FARM 28/M 20 a 15.80	
	4		New line laid to 21 Bde & lateral communication established between them & 89 Bde.	
	5,6,7,8		Salvage parties found & general maintenance	
	9		do	
	10		do	
	11		do	
	12		Ruin in KEMMEL Area explored & work begun for their recovery. Salvage took to vicinity of MONT VIDAIGNE. Work in KEMMEL continued. do do	

WAR DIARY
or
INTELLIGENCE SUMMARY.

(Erase heading not required.)

Army Form C. 2118.

Place	Date	Hour	Summary of Events and Information	Remarks and references to Appendices
MONT VIDAIGNE	13		Lieut. E.A. ASHMORE R.E. (T) joined Coy. from 2nd Army Sig. Coy. R.E	
	14		Work on new office for Officers at MONT NOIR CHATEAU. New laterals laid to Right & Left Divisions	
	15		Div. HQ at SOVIET FARM closed Sam. + opened at MONT NOIR CHATEAU 11.0 am. Cables from CRITERION to SUMP holes.	
	16		Salvage + continuous work at new HQ.	
	17		Work on test-point BB - MD - K3 in KEMMEL Brewery. Lieut F.M. LORD R.E. left on 14 days leave to England.	
	18		Starts to take over front from 36 Division.	
	19		90 Bde moves into line. HQ at CRUCIFIX CORNER. Lieut E.A. ASHMORE on 14 days leave to ENGLAND.	
	20		Salvage	
	21		Buries in Right Sector explored, + three pairs taken into use to HILL 63	
	22		Salvage Rear Div. HQ moved to S. JANS CHATEAU.	
	23		Reserve Bde to S. JANS CHATEAU + MONT NOIR CAMP.	
	24		do	
	25		do	
	26		Two lines laid to Adv. HQ. of left Bde at ARMOUR FARM	
	27		Two lines laid to CL Test-Point for new position of 90 Bde. 90 Bde moves to DE MENNEBUCK SIDING (DM Test Point) Left Bde moves to Tyre Farm from BEAVER HALL.	
	28		Adv. HQ closes at TYRD FARM. LEFT BDE moves to ARMOUR FARM.	
	29			
	30		Lines laid to WYTSCHAETE + NORTE WILDE for new positions.	

No. 36

30TH DIVISIONAL SIGNAL COMPANY – ROYAL ENGINEERS.

W A R   D I A R Y

for the month of

OCTOBER, 1918.

VOLUMN XXXVI.

1-11-18.

S. Hagarramp
Major, R.E.
O.C. 30th Divisional Signal Coy. R.E.

Army Form C. 2118

WAR DIARY
or
INTELLIGENCE SUMMARY

(Erase heading not required.)

Instructions regarding War Diaries and Intelligence Summaries are contained in F.S. Regs., Part II. and the Staff Manual respectively. Title Pages will be prepared in manuscript.

Place	Date	Hour	Summary of Events and Information	Remarks and references to Appendices
VIGNACOURT	2nd		Headquarters & No. 1 Section left VIGNACOURT at 9 a.m. on the 3rd instant, arriving at ALLONVILLE at 1 p.m. the same day, where the Company went into billets.	
ALLONVILLE	3rd		Headquarters & No. 1 Section left ALLONVILLE at 9 a.m. on the 4th instant, for BUIRE, where they arrived at 4-30 p.m. the same day and went into billets.	
BUIRE.	4th to 10th.		Headquarters & No. 1 Section left BUIRE at 8 a.m. on the 11th instant, arriving at FRICOURT at 11-45 a.m. the same day. Accommodation for the men was found in dugouts, hutments and tents.	
FRICOURT.	11th to 21st.		Sub-Offices were opened at FERRET TRENCH (S.6.a.5/9) and E.11 Central. Advanced Divisional Headquarters were established at CARLTON TRENCH (S.16.b.2/3), a point WEST of LONGUEVAL, at 1 p.m. on the 17th instant.	
			The following are notes on operations during the period 11th to 21st instant inclusive:-	
			TELEPHONIC AND TELEGRAPHIC.	
			Communication was at all times well maintained. During the whole period of operations communication was never lost to the Brigades, but great difficulty was experienced in maintaining the lines, which were very frequently cut. It was necessary at times to have as many as six lines to ensure communication at all.	
			WIRELESS.	
			Wireless was used with success. Over 100 messages were sent during operations. This method of communication proved good.	
			PIGEONS.	
			Pigeons were again used with great success. As on previous occasions, the first message to arrive from the front line after the attack had been launched was by Carrier Pigeon.	

Army Form C. 2118

WAR DIARY
or
INTELLIGENCE SUMMARY

SHEET 2.

(Erase heading not required.)

Instructions regarding War Diaries and Intelligence Summaries are contained in F. S. Regs., Part II. and the Staff Manual respectively. Title Pages will be prepared in manuscript.

Place	Date	Hour	Summary of Events and Information	Remarks and references to Appendices
FRICOURT	11th to 21st.		**VISUAL.** Four stations comprising the visual system were manned during the whole period of operations, but were never used. **RUNNERS.** The usual system of "runners" was employed, and was satisfactory. The state of the trenches, however, such as they were, made great delay in this service. **DESPATCH RIDERS.** The roads were entirely impassable for motor cyclists, and Horse Despatch Riders had invariably to be used for work forward of FRICOURT.	
RIBEMONT	22nd to 24th.		Headquarters & No. 1 Section left FRICOURT at 9 a.m. on the 22nd instant, arriving at RIBEMONT at 4 p.m. the same day, where the Company went into billets.	
TALMAS	25th.		Headquarters & No. 1 Section left RIBEMONT for TALMAS at 5-15 a.m. on the 25th instant, at which place they arrived 10-30 a.m. the same day, and stayed overnight.	
PAS.	26th to 30th		Headquarters & No. 1 Section resumed journey to PAS at 8-30 a.m. on the 26th instant, reaching their destination at 1-30 p.m the same day.	
BAVINCOURT	31st	10-30 a.m.	Company left PAS for BAVINCOURT at 8 a.m. on the 31st instant, arriving there 10-30 a.m. the same day. We took over the Office from the 46th Divisional Signal Company at 10 a.m. on the 31st instant. One Cable Section detached during whole month with 30th Divisional Artillery.	

Army Form C. 2118.

WAR DIARY
or
INTELLIGENCE SUMMARY.
(Erase heading not required.)

Instructions regarding War Diaries and Intelligence Summaries are contained in F.S. Regs., Part II. and the Staff Manual respectively. Title pages will be prepared in manuscript.

OCTOBER

Place	Date	Hour	Summary of Events and Information	Remarks and references to Appendices
WYTSCHAETE AREA	1		Adv. Div. HQ. closed at TYRO FARM & moved forward to NORTEWULDE, thence to LUMM FARM, where new office was established. His Lair to be at HUTHEM. Wireless Mast most useful.	
	2		Adv. Div. closed at LUMM FARM. Lt/Whr. E.R. BALDWIN R.E. at 11h/Whr. R. BALDWIN R.E. at 22h/P19C 14 Sept. left to joined at LAMPPOST CORNER (WYTSCHAETE) and to Isle at 22h/P19C 1:3. Lineman's post formed near RIDGE FARM. Rear Echlon from MONT NOIR to TYRO FARM. Rear to NORFOLK CAMP.	
	3			
	4		Maintenance	
	5			
	6		Capt. C.T. CROWSWICK R.E. proceeded on 1 month's leave to ENGLAND. Lieut. E.A. ASHMORE R.E. returns from leave.	
	7		Lieut R. WATKINS-PITCHFORD R.E. to Hospital. Line laid to HUTHEM (Right Tho) along old BELGIAN STATE RAILWAY TRACK.	
	8		One of the lines along WYTSCHAETE-OSTAVERNE-HUTHEM fixed reels up. Lineman's post moved to Isle HQ at 22h/P19C. Wireless section removed from NORFOLK CAMP.	
	9		New line laid to Div HQ. Right at WULVERGHEM. Line from TYRO FARM reels up.	
	10		Maintenance	
	11			
	12			
	13		10 p.m. Wireless Mast - Truck to New Line to Rear HQ via Spur line to LITTLE KEMMEL. Attack commenced. New line to left Bde from LITTLE KEMMEL Fords. Line will be up after attack.	
	14			

WAR DIARY
or
INTELLIGENCE SUMMARY.
(Erase heading not required.)

Army Form C. 2118.

Place	Date	Hour	Summary of Events and Information	Remarks and references to Appendices
Wytschaete Area.	Oct 15		Transport moved from Norfolk Camp to 28/I/a.6.9. Rear Office at TYRO FARM closed down & opened at 28/N/18.6.3.5 at 23.00. D3 Cable laid from Adv. Div HQ to 28/N/18.6.3.5. Loop sets proved extremely useful at this time, communication being kept with Bns throughout the attack by this means.	
Kastewilde Area	16.		Remainder of rear echelon moved to WYTSCHAETE. Rev HQ closes at TYRO FARM. Advanced Post opened at TRAMLINE FARM 28/Q/14.6.54. Rear Office moved fm 28/N/18.6.3.5 to ZANDST CORNER. 90 Div took over front fm RH DR of 34 Div, with HQs at 28/Q/9.a.1.1. 1/Lieut. E. HANCOCK reported as Supernumerary Officer fm 2nd Army Sig Co. R.E. Adv. HQ moved during afternoon to farm at 28/Q/13 d.Y.Y. Rear Office moves to TRALEE FARM.	
Werwick Area	17			
	18		One Cable Detachment - now w/Lieut E. HANCOCK RE. attached to 90 Bde to maintain communication during advance. One operator + D.R. Motor Cyclist forms Mobile HQ in attendance on G.O.C., in line of Communication. Transport moves fm WYTSCHAETE to Adv. Div. HQ.	
Ronca and Croise	19.		So Div HQs closes at 11.00. These Gov HQs moved to TRALEE FARM & opens at LABLAERS CROSSROADS. Advic at 11.00. These Gov HQs moved to CROISE (R 36 a.1.5) at 13.15. Advic forms at 28/Q 24.6.9.1.	

Army Form C. 2118.

WAR DIARY
INTELLIGENCE SUMMARY.
(Erase heading not required.)

Instructions regarding War Diaries and Intelligence Summaries are contained in F. S. Regs., Part II. and the Staff Manual respectively. Title pages will be prepared in manuscript.

Place	Date	Hour	Summary of Events and Information	Remarks and references to Appendices
CROISÉ and STERHOEK	20.		1st Lieut. G.R. COCHRAN R.E. proceeded on 14 days special leave to U.K. Div. and Sig. Transpt. moved to STERHOEK. Rear HQ. closed at CROISÉ and moved to STERHOEK.	
COYGHEM.	21.			
	22.		Cav. Div. HQ. opened at COYGHEM	
	23.		Lt. R.W. RICHARDS R.E. rejoined from Hospital	
	24.		1st Lieut. F.M. LORD R.E. to Hospital	Remained – line replaces back cable lines, it carries risk of being there days.
	25.		Lines laid to 14 Div at DOTTIGNIES	
	26.		Lines Cav. 13 to Bde on Left. Forward line to Middle Div. HQ. maintained.	
	27.		Lines extended to new positions at 2/1 Bde. 1st Lieut. T.G.M. MALAN R.E. joined for duty from 2nd Army Sig. Coy. R.E. as supernumerary, was attached to 2/1 Bde. Section. 1st Lieut. E. HANCOCK R.E. and detachment opens HQ. to forward Bde.	
	28.		Lines laid to new positions of 89 Bde. at RUDDERVORDE. Lateral put through to 35, 36, and 41 Divs. Lieut. W. BAKER, WORCESTER REGT. joined in July as supernumerary from 2nd Army Sig. Coy. R.E., was attached to 2/46 Bde. R.F.A. Salvage Maintenance Cav.Div.HQ. moved back to ROLLEGHEM. Sigs. Transpt. moved to RULLEGHEM under 1st Lieut. E. HANCOCK R.E.	
	29 to 30. 31.			

S. Fazakerley, Major R.E.
O.C. 3rd Div. Sig. Coy. R.E.

SECRET.

30TH DIVISIONAL SIGNAL COMPANY - ROYAL ENGINEERS.

W A R   D I A R Y

for the month of

NOVEMBER, 1918.

VOLUME XXVII.

Vol 37

[signature]
Capt., R.E.
for O.C. 30th Divisional Signal Coy. R.E.

1-12-18.

WAR DIARY

INTELLIGENCE SUMMARY.

Army Form C. 2118.

Place	Date	Hour	Summary of Events and Information	Remarks and references to Appendices
ROLLEGHEM	1		Line laid to Bde HQ at -29/O 36 c 7.5. Six miles D5 cable salved in COYGHEM Area.	
	2		Lt. J.W. WRIGHT, Gen. List, to Div. HQ for attachment to 'G' on Staff Liaison. Lieut. E. HANCOCK R.E. to 90 Bde. for temporary duty as Bde. Sig. Officer. Single line laid to BELLEGHEM, making existing circuit metallic. Line to HERBAU FARM reeled in.	
	3		Salvage ammunition.	
BELLEGHEM	4		Rear HQ closed at STERNDEK 09.00 hours, & Div. HQ closed at ROLLEGHEM 14.00 hours. New HQ Office established at BELLEGHEM. Transport moved to BELLEGHEM at 09.30 hours under O.S.M., line laid to Bg. Pte. YE 2355 split at BELLEGHEM, Rear portion working to Tran + D.A.D.O.S. forward portion used as lateral to Div. on right.	
	5		Lieut. G.G. COCHRAN R.E. injured for special duties, line laid to GAII CABT. (29/O 32 & 45.05) for 21 Bde. This m.s. was cancelled.	
	6		Line continued from GAII CABT. to VANDSMOLLE FARM (29/O 33 a 8.7) for 89 Bde. Line laid from KNOCHE m.s. to KNOCHE 10 m.s. to Te-in was run for the 11th D.A. for work from 29/O 29 a 7.6 to YC 14 on main KNOCHE - MOEN road. Detail of line laid to Bde, N Div. on &F (YC 17.)	

WAR DIARY or INTELLIGENCE SUMMARY

Army Form C. 2118.

Place	Date	Hour	Summary of Events and Information	Remarks and references to Appendices
	7.		90 Bde moved from the line into rest at 29/N.15 d 4.8. YC17 split at their office. Line to train at ROLLEGHEM taken up by us as lateral to 29 Div. Train moved to AELBEKE, line from 29 Div. Exchange & then YC16 continued from 29/O 21 d 20.05 to 89 Bde at KNOCKE. Line runs from 89 Bde to 200, 201, 202 Field Coys R.E. to Russian Batts. YC 20 runs from X Corps Heavier Cavalry Batty. R.C. at 29/O 20 a 9.2 to 89 Bde & connected in All BA Bde on Right. Salvage parties at work.	
HEESTERT	8.		Cable Detachment under Lieut. G.O. COCHRAN R.E. sent to 89 Bde & lay forward line during advance and laid from KNOCKE to AUTRYVE. Adv. Div. Hd. moved to HEESTERT.	
WATREPONT	9.		Pontoon bridge across R. ESCAULT at ESCANAFFLES completed being at 40 a.m. line (YC 90) was continued to 29/X 30 c 80.15, when 89 Bde. Hqrs. were established for night Nov 10/11. Adv. Div. Hd moved to WATREPONT. Rear Adv. to HEESTERT. YC 90 line from existing cable-head to BIERCAMP (outpost line) 30/U 26 c 5.3. Adv. Div Hd moved to ELLEZELLES.	
ELLEZELLES	10.			
	11.	11.00	ARMISTICE DECLARED.	
	12.		Rear Div HQ moved to RENAIX. Forward detachment rejoined, working with YC 90 from BIERCAMP to FLOBECQ en route.	

Army Form C. 2118.

WAR DIARY
INTELLIGENCE SUMMARY.
(Erase heading not required.)

Instructions regarding War Diaries and Intelligence Summaries are contained in F.S. Regs., Part II. and the Staff Manual respectively. Title pages will be prepared in manuscript.

Place	Date	Hour	Summary of Events and Information	Remarks and references to Appendices
	13.		Sg Bde moved from FLOBECQ to RENAIX. YC 90 rode in from FLOBECQ to ELLEZELLES. Open routes between ELLEZELLES and outpost line reconnoitred.	
	14.		" " RENAIX	
	15.		Q.W. Div. HQqrs closed at ELLEZELLES 12.00 & opened at MOUSCRON at same hour. Transport moved by road, leaving 01.00 hours.	
MOUSCRON	16.		Remainder of Div HQqrs. moved from RENAIX to MOUSCRON. Transport - lines in wood from MOUSCRON Station to VALERIA FARM 29/5 28 c 1.8.	
	17.		Overhauling of wagons, checking of stores.	
	18.		Physical Training, speeding, sheathing & maintenance	
	19.		" "	
	20.		" "	
	21.		" "	
	22.		" "	
	23.		" "	Major E KAYE PARRY R.E. to U.K on 14 Days leave.
	24.		" "	
	25.		" "	
	26.		" "	
	27.		" "	
	28.		Wireless Stations established at FUNQUEREAU, LA GORGUE and ST. VENANT - staging places on line of march - to keep communication with Brigades while in move. Advance party sent to RENESCURE	

WAR DIARY
INTELLIGENCE SUMMARY

Army Form C. 2118.

Place	Date	Hour	Summary of Events and Information	Remarks and references to Appendices
	29.		Physical Training, operating & maintenance, Wagons loaded. Preparations for move.	
	30.		Transport moved off under Lieut. G.G. COCHRAN R.E. at 07.00 hours, and stayed for night at ERQUINGHEM. 'A' & 'D' Wanders moved to RENESCURE. Officers relief moved by lorry to new office	

C.M. Clement
Capt. R.E.
for D.C° 30 Div. Sig. Coy. RE.

Secret.

30th Divisional Signal Company - Royal Engineers.

WAR DIARY
for the month of
DECEMBER, 1918.

VOLUMN XXXVlll.

E. Page Payns.
Major R.E.
30th Division Signal Coy. R.E.

1-1-19.

Army Form C. 2118.

WAR DIARY
or
INTELLIGENCE SUMMARY.
(Erase heading not required.)

30th Div. Signal C.R.E.

December 1918.

Place	Date	Hour	Summary of Events and Information	Remarks and references to Appendices
MOUSCRON	1		Transport stages Nieuwelberge area – Office opened RENESCURE A&Q	
RENESCURE	2		Office closed MOUSCRON. Rear party moved to RENESCURE. Reinforcements arrived A/Pm.	
	3.		Div. Rough lines to all Brigades as follows:- HQ at BLARINGHEM, 21st Bde at WARDRECQUES, 89th Bde at WALLON CAPPEL, 90th Bde at STEENBECQUE, M.G. Battalion at STAPLES, 89th Bde recharge opened.	
	4.		21st Bde recharge opened. – D.A. recharge established BLARINGHEM.	
	5.		90th Bde recharge opened. Communications arranged to RFA Bdes and all field Coys at AIRE and Pioneers at EBBLINGHEM.	
	6.		Commenced work on new Signal Camp. Education, parading and miniature	
	7.		Continued " " " "	
	8.		Lt. C.G. COCHRAN to England for duty	
	9.		Work on new Signal Camp. Education, parades and miniature	
	10.		" " " " "	
	11.		" " " " "	

Army Form C. 2118.

WAR DIARY
or
INTELLIGENCE SUMMARY
(Erase heading not required.)

30 Divi. Signal Co. R.E. / Cash

Dec. 1918 / Cash

Place	Date	Hour	Summary of Events and Information	Remarks and references to Appendices
RENESCURE	12		Party to Signal Camp - Operating and Maintenance - Lieut MALAN proceeds to 6 Division Hd.Qrs.	
	13		Salvage party reported 66 Labour Group for work to forward areas - Work in Signal Camp - Operating and Maintenance	
	14		" " " " " " "	
	15		" " " " " " "	
	16		" " " " " " "	
	17		Medal parade - G.O.C. presented medals to 6:- ____, 1 Officer, 4 N.C.O.s and 8 men of this Company - Operating and Maintenance	
	18		Work in Camp - Operating and Maintenance	
			Carbide lighting system established	
	19		Work in Signal Camp - Operating and Maintenance	
	20		" " " " " " "	
	21		" " " " " " "	
	22		" " " " " " "	
	23		" " " " " " "	
			Salvage party reported 66 Labour Group (about 120 men) with working other units	

Army Form C. 2118.

WAR DIARY
or
INTELLIGENCE SUMMARY.
(Erase heading not required.)

20th A.S. Signal Co. E.G. Dec 1918 (Cont)

Instructions regarding War Diaries and Intelligence Summaries are contained in F. S. Regs., Part II. and the Staff Manual respectively. Title pages will be prepared in manuscript.

Place	Date	Hour	Summary of Events and Information	Remarks and references to Appendices
RENESCURE	24		Work in signed Camp - Operating and Maintenance -	
	25		Christmas Day -	
	26		Boxing Day	
	27		Work in signed Camp -	
	28		" " " "	Lieut MALAN
	29		Work in signed Camp - Operating and Maintenance	"
	30		Classification of lines & wires by S.B.O.S. Relaying all superfluous lab to Dump. Ready to parish wire.	"
	31		Work in Cable wagon	"

SECRET.

30th. DIVISIONAL SIGNAL COMPANY - ROYAL ENGINEERS.

WAR DIARY.
for the month of
JANUARY 1919.

VOLUME XXXIX

E. Kaye Parry.
Major R.E.
30th: Divisional Signal Company R.E.

1/2/19

Army Form C. 2118.

WAR DIARY
or
INTELLIGENCE SUMMARY.
(Erase heading not required)

3D Div Signal Coy RE   January 1919.

Place	Date	Hour	Summary of Events and Information	Remarks and references to Appendices
RENESCURE	1-3		Maintenance and General Camp duties	
"	4		Horse and Harness inspection by O.C.Coy	
"	5-9		Maintenance and General Camp duties	
"	10.		" 2/Lt J.G.H. MILAN transferred to UK	
"	11.		Checking stores & transport readiness for move	
"	12.		Dismantling flag & lighting system. Advance party to LA CAPELLE	
"	13		1st Tr. PERE proceeded on leave to UK. No 2 with Signal office staff	
"			moved by motor lorry up to LA CAPELLE. No 3 Section	
LA CAPELLE	14		with Transport detailed march off by road at 7 o'clock arrived at BAVENGHEM	
"			# left BAVENGHEM at 7 o'clock arrived at BELLE	
BELLE	15		No 1 Section & transport rested at BELLE ready to move to suitable billets	
COLEMBERT	16		" moved to Heard Army August School COLEMBERT Horse	
"			L.O. taken ill & moved	
"	17		Hr. Qrs. moved to COLEMBERT. Signal Office & Staff Billeted in LA CAPELLE	
"	18		Work on Horse and Wagon lines	
"	19		" Lt W.BAKER leave to UK. Have LO sick	

Army Form C. 2118.

WAR DIARY
or
INTELLIGENCE SUMMARY.
(Erase heading not required.)

30th Div Signal Coy R.E.   January 1917

Place	Date	Hour	Summary of Events and Information	Remarks and references to Appendices
COLEMBERT	20-21-22		Transfer over & general camp Routine	
	23		L't E.A ASHMORE proceeded on leave to UK	
	24		"	
	25		Cpt. D.A Hd Qrs & horse also 2nd Bgd &	
			3rd wire parties joined Coy at COLEMBERT from BLARINGHEM and WIRE respectively	
	26		Instruction & general camp routine	
	27		"	
	28		Examination and reclassification of animals by Remount Board	
	29		Transferred to general camp Routine	
	30		L't C.A WEBSTER proceeded on leave to UK	
	31		"	

SECRET.

30th Divisional Signal Company- Royal Engineers.

WAR DIARY.

for the month of

FEBRUARY 1919

VOLUME XXXX

[signature] /h Major R.E.

30th Divisional Signal Coy R.E.

1-3-19.

Army Form C. 2118.

WAR DIARY
or
INTELLIGENCE SUMMARY.

(Erase heading not required.)

30th Div. Signal Coy. R.E.

February 1919

Place	Date	Hour	Summary of Events and Information	Remarks and references to Appendices
Colembert	1		Operating demobilisation camp signal exchanges and camp routine	
	2		" Lt. W. Baker rejoined from leave to U.K.	
	3		" and camp routine	
	4		" "	
	5		" "	
	6		" Capt. C.T. Cranswick proceeded on leave to U.K.	
	7		" and camp routine	
	8		" Lt. G.R.J. Watkins-Pitchford to hospital sick	
	9		" and camp routine	
	10		" "	
	11		" Lt. R.J. Peake rejoined from leave to U.K.	
	12		" and camp routine	
	13		" "	
	14		Lt. L.H.P. Ibbotson proceeded on leave to U.K. Lt. E.A. Ashmore rejoined from leave to U.K.	
	15		Operating demobilisation camp signal exchanges and camp routine	

WAR DIARY
or
INTELLIGENCE SUMMARY.

30th DIV. SIGNAL COY. R.E.   FEBRUARY 1919

Place	Date	Hour	Summary of Events and Information	Remarks and references to Appendices
COLEMBERT	16		Operating demobilisation camp exchange. Lt. G.R.J. WATKINS-PITCHFORD rejoined from hospital	
	17		and camp routine	
	18		"	
	19		"	
	20		CAPT. C.T. CRANSWICK rejoined from leave to U.K.	
	21		" and camp routine	
	22		"	
	23		"	
	24		Advance party proceeded to CONDETTE to establish signal office	
	25		Lt. C.D. WEBSTER rejoined from leave to U.K.	
	26		Signal office moved from LA CAPELLE to CONDETTE	
	27		General camp routine. Animals demobilised from 1st of March. 12 RIDERS, 7 L.D. HORSES + MULES. Lt. L.H.P. IBBOTSON rejoined from leave to U.K.	
	28		General camp routine	

SECRET.

30TH DIVISIONAL SIGNAL COMPANY - ROYAL ENGINEERS.

W A R   D I A R Y

for the month of

MARCH - 1919.

VOLUMN xxxxl.

[signature]
Captain, R.E.
O.C. 30th Divisional Signal Coy. R.E.

1-4-19.

Army Form C. 2118.

30th DIV. SIGNAL Coy. R.E. WAR DIARY or INTELLIGENCE SUMMARY.

MARCH 1919

(Erase heading not required.)

Instructions regarding War Diaries and Intelligence Summaries are contained in F. S. Regs., Part II. and the Staff Manual respectively. Title pages will be prepared in manuscript.

Place	Date	Hour	Summary of Events and Information	Remarks and references to Appendices
COLOMBERT	1		Operating demobilisation camp signal exchange & general camp writer	
	2		Lt. E.L. Osborne proceeds to Div. H.Q. at least to appointed signals office	
	3		Operating demobilisation camp signal exchange and general camp writer	
	4		" "	
	5		" "	
	6		" "	
	7		Major E. Kaye-Parry proceeded on leave to U.K.	
	8		Operating demobilisation camp signal exchange and general camp writer	
	9		" "	
	10		" "	
	11		" "	
	12		" "	
CHOQUEL	13		Headquarters and two Colombert to Choquel (Haudelot)	
	13		transport to No. 10. Vet. Hospital at Neufchatel	
	14		Operating signal exchange. Camp changes writer	
	15		" "	

30th DIV. SIGNAL COY. R.E. WAR DIARY or INTELLIGENCE SUMMARY.

Army Form C. 2118.

MARCH 1919

Place	Date	Hour	Summary of Events and Information	Remarks and references to Appendices
CHOQUEL (HARDELOT)	16		Sending signal exchanges & general camp routine	
	17		"	
	18		"	
	19		"	
	20		"	
	21		"	
	22		Capt R.W. NEWMAN, M.C., proceeded on leave to U.K.	
	23		Sending signal exchanges & general camp routine	
	24		"	
	25		"	
	26		Maj. E. KAYE-PARRY returned from leave to U.K.	
	27		Sending signal exchanges & general camp routine	
	28		Maj. E. KAYE-PARRY proceeded to No 5. AREA SIGS. LILLE as O.C. Signals	
	29		Lt. G.R.L. WATKINS-PITCHFORD proceeded on leave to U.K.	
	30		Sending signal exchanges & general camp routine	
	31		"	

WM 42

SECRET.

30TH DIVISIONAL SIGNAL COMPANY - ROYAL ENGINEERS.

WAR DIARY

for the month of

APRIL 1919.

VOLUME XL11.

[signature]
Captain R.E.,
O.C. 30th Divisional Signal Coy. R.E.

1-5-19.

30th Div Signal Coy R.E.

Army Form C. 2118.

WAR DIARY
or
INTELLIGENCE SUMMARY.
(Erase heading not required.)

April 1919

Instructions regarding War Diaries and Intelligence Summaries are contained in F. S. Regs., Part II. and the Staff Manual respectively. Title pages will be prepared in manuscript.

Place	Date	Hour	Summary of Events and Information	Remarks and references to Appendices
Choques	1		Signal office duties - (operating signal exchange) + general camp duties routine	
Coudette	2		"	
	3		"	
	4		"	
	5		"	
	6		"	
	7		"	
	8		"	
	9		"	
	10		"	
	11		"	
	12		Moved from Coudette to Choques (Nordelot) Choques to Coudette	
Coudette	13		Operating signal exchange + general camp routine	
	14		Capt. R.W. Thurman MC. returned from leave 32 arrivals to Account Depot for demobilization had to return N.E. to N.C.O's & O.R. 2 destined the following before N.E. to U.K. for dispersal	

3rd R.W. Signal Coy. R.E.

Army Form C. 2118.

WAR DIARY
or
INTELLIGENCE SUMMARY.
(Erase heading not required.)

April 1919

Place	Date	Hour	Summary of Events and Information	Remarks and references to Appendices
Roulette	15		Sergt. Ed Calman R.E. to 10th Bra Signals - Lille - to duty.	
	16		Lieut. H.J. Mathews Pickford R.E. to U.K. for dispersal	
			Capt. R.W. Newman Rule to Eastern Gil Signal Coy. Rhine Army - to duty	
	17		7 arrivals to 10th Remount depot for demobilization	
	18		Operating signal exchange & general camp routine	
	19		1 arrival to 10th Remount depot for demobilization	
	20		Operating signal exchange & general camp routine	
	21		Lieut. G.A. Webster to U.K. for dispersal	
	22		Operating signal exchange & general camp routine	
	23		Lieut. F.W. Thorton from 2nd Inf. Bde Sigs to Coy Hqrs to duty.	
	24		1 arrival to 10th Remount depot for demobilization	
	25		Operating signal exchange & general camp routine	
	26		4 arrivals to 10th Remount depot for demobilization	
	27		Operating signal exchange & general camp duties	
	28		" " " " "	
	29		" " " " "	
	30		Capt. R.W. Newman Rule ceded on leave to U.K.	

30th Divn. "A".

Herewith War Diary for the month of May 1919.

Lieut.
O.C. 30th Divl. Signal Coy. R.E.

6-6-19.

Army Form C. 2118.

WAR DIARY
or
INTELLIGENCE SUMMARY.
(Erase heading not required.)

WL 443

Place	Date	Hour	Summary of Events and Information	Remarks and references to Appendices
Boudette	1	—	Christmas signal exchange & general census routine	
	2		" "	
	3		" "	
	4		" "	
	5		" "	5.9 temp to camp
	6		" "	2 Horses Tetanus
	7		" "	
	8		" "	
	9		" "	
	10		" "	2horses 24/10
	11		" "	
	12		" "	
	13		" "	
	14		Capt. 1st. commands to the R.E. Winchester for 16/4 exhibition. H. Webster lost in camp	
	15		Starting pigeon exchange civil camp .	
	16		Lieut W. Baker serine from Court to UK	

Instructions regarding War Diaries and Intelligence Summaries are contained in F. S. Regs., Part II. and the Staff Manual respectively. Title pages will be prepared in manuscript.

Army Form C. 2118.

WAR DIARY
or
INTELLIGENCE SUMMARY.
(Erase heading not required.)

Place	Date	Hour	Summary of Events and Information	Remarks and references to Appendices
CONDETTE	17		Operating signal exchange + general camp routine	
	18			
	19			– 2.D to N.4 Bn – a
	20			
	21			
	22			– 2.D ditto
	23			
	24			
	25			
	26			
	27			– A.Pilon ditto
	28		SIGNAL Stores detached to SIGNAL Park, CALAIS – (Gratuitous) – Chambers Sgt. BALLOCK NE	
	29			
	30		Operating Signal Exchange + General Camp routine All those transport in charge of this unit handed over to M.M.C.S. R.E. BALLOCK NE	
	31			

www.ingramcontent.com/pod-product-compliance
Lightning Source LLC
Chambersburg PA
CBHW081402160426
43193CB00013B/2088